THE COOPERATIVE LEARNING GUIDE & PLANNING PAK FOR MIDDLE GRADES

Thematic Projects & Activities

by Imogene Forte
and
Sandra Schurr

Incentive Publications, Inc.
Nashville, Tennessee

Cover by Terrence Donaldson
Illustrations by Marta Johnson
Edited by Jan Keeling

ISBN 0-86530-199-9

TABLE OF CONTENTS

Thematic Poster Projects

Teacher's Tool Kit

How To Use This Book

In today's fast-paced and rapidly changing world, teachers are faced with the awesome task of preparing students to function effectively in an ever more complex and demanding society. Curriculum development and daily lesson planning can become an almost overwhelming challenge as teachers attempt to give proper weight to advances in technology, global awareness, environmental consciousness, basic skills and concept development, and personal responsibility.

The Cooperative Learning Guide & Planning Pak for Middle Grades/Thematic Projects and Activities has been developed to help teachers meet these all-encompassing demands. It has been our purpose to pull together and organize research-based information, tried-and-true teaching strategies, and high-interest skills-based activities to make lesson planning and classroom management easier and more meaningful.

Collaboration is the key concept for success in the 21st century, whether in business, in government, or in international affairs. Teamwork has become the norm for getting positive results in the family structure, in the workplace, and in the globalization of the world. The Information Age demands that one be able to function in group settings of all sizes so that all involved can adapt to the phenomenon of rapid change and the complexity of technology.

A tried-and-true method for promoting cooperative learning in the classroom is afforded through the use of thematic interdisciplinary units. For years teachers have planned and implemented thematic units to encourage small, large, and total group discussion and brainstorming, as well as to provide opportunities for cooperative planning, goal setting, task completion, and evaluation of shared learning expectancies. When these units are structured so that they are interdisciplinary in nature, including a variety of activities ranging across the content spectrum, cooperative learning possibilities and student motivation are enhanced.

The materials in *The Cooperative Learning Guide & Planning Pak for Middle Grades/Thematic Projects and Activities* have been organized in the following manner to allow for ready reference and ease of use.

- **Teacher's Overview of Cooperative Learning and Thematic Teaching** utilizes a simple question-and-answer format to clarify major issues related to cooperative learning and thematic units.

- **Reference Skills Sharpeners** are thematic units designed to introduce cooperative learning strategies and techniques and to encourage and strengthen everyday use of reference materials.

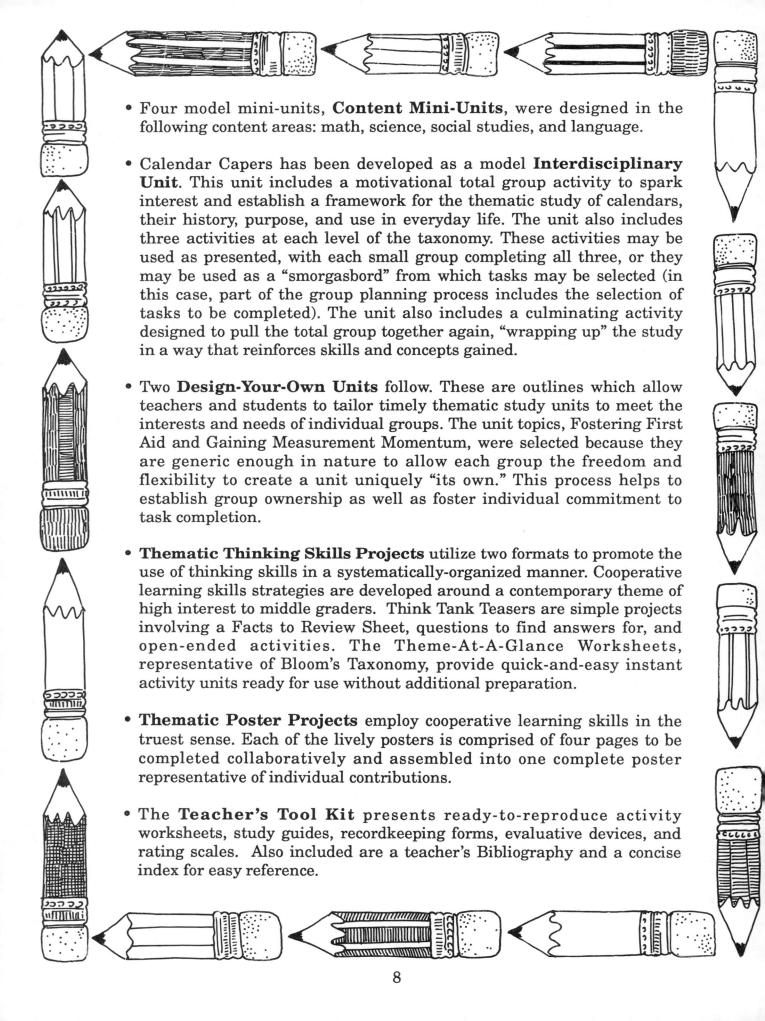

- Four model mini-units, **Content Mini-Units**, were designed in the following content areas: math, science, social studies, and language.

- Calendar Capers has been developed as a model **Interdisciplinary Unit**. This unit includes a motivational total group activity to spark interest and establish a framework for the thematic study of calendars, their history, purpose, and use in everyday life. The unit also includes three activities at each level of the taxonomy. These activities may be used as presented, with each small group completing all three, or they may be used as a "smorgasbord" from which tasks may be selected (in this case, part of the group planning process includes the selection of tasks to be completed). The unit also includes a culminating activity designed to pull the total group together again, "wrapping up" the study in a way that reinforces skills and concepts gained.

- Two **Design-Your-Own Units** follow. These are outlines which allow teachers and students to tailor timely thematic study units to meet the interests and needs of individual groups. The unit topics, Fostering First Aid and Gaining Measurement Momentum, were selected because they are generic enough in nature to allow each group the freedom and flexibility to create a unit uniquely "its own." This process helps to establish group ownership as well as foster individual commitment to task completion.

- **Thematic Thinking Skills Projects** utilize two formats to promote the use of thinking skills in a systematically-organized manner. Cooperative learning skills strategies are developed around a contemporary theme of high interest to middle graders. Think Tank Teasers are simple projects involving a Facts to Review Sheet, questions to find answers for, and open-ended activities. The Theme-At-A-Glance Worksheets, representative of Bloom's Taxonomy, provide quick-and-easy instant activity units ready for use without additional preparation.

- **Thematic Poster Projects** employ cooperative learning skills in the truest sense. Each of the lively posters is comprised of four pages to be completed collaboratively and assembled into one complete poster representative of individual contributions.

- The **Teacher's Tool Kit** presents ready-to-reproduce activity worksheets, study guides, recordkeeping forms, evaluative devices, and rating scales. Also included are a teacher's Bibliography and a concise index for easy reference.

1. What Is Cooperative Learning?

Cooperative learning differs from other types of small-group instruction in that it is comprised of five basic elements identified by Johnson and Johnson (1986). These include:

- Positive interdependence whereby students recognize that their mutual success must be a collaborative effort.

- Individual accountability whereby students are accountable for their own mastery of the material presented as well as for that of the entire group.

- Face-to-face interaction among students which allows them to summarize and elaborate on materials being studied and to extend concepts and skills being learned.

- Appropriate use of collaborative skills.

- Use of social skills to determine the degree of group effectiveness.

2. How Does One Group Students For Cooperative Learning?

Group sizes can vary in number from two to six, depending on the nature of the assignment. One should keep in mind, however, that the smaller the group, the more active participation is likely to occur among group members. For example, in a group of two, each student is potentially active 50 percent of the time, while students in groups of four are potentially active 25 percent of the time. This is especially true during group discussions.

Students should generally be grouped heterogeneously to achieve diversity in gender, ability levels, socio-economic levels, interest areas, and ethnic backgrounds. One might make an exception to this guideline when forming groups for specific skill development. Three methods can be used for placing students in groups. These are:

- Organization by the teacher, using a rank-ordering procedure. The teacher will use test scores, grades, or achievement levels to place students; the goal is a balance of low, medium, and high scores/levels within each group.

- Random organization, achieved by drawing names out of a hat, or having students count off by fours (or threes, sixes, etc.).

- Organization by students on occasion. Student selection of groups should follow ground rules, such as mixed gender or race, that have been specified by the teacher.

Often randomly-organized groups provide the best opportunities for results, because they are perceived as being most "fair" by the students, because they generate unusual combinations of students, and because they require students to work with everyone in the class at one time or another.

3. What Kinds Of Roles Should Be Assigned To Students In Groups?

It is important that every group member be assigned a role for every activity. These roles should be determined by the learning task. The following are some roles to consider:

- **Coordinator/Manager** keeps the group on task.

- **Timekeeper** keeps track of time allotted for assignments.

- **Secretary/Recorder** writes down group responses.

- **Evaluator** keeps notes on group processing and social skills.

- **Encourager** makes sure all group members have their turns.

- **Reader** reads directions, problems, and resource materials to all group members.

- **Checker** checks for group members' comprehension of material to be learned or discussed.

- **Praiser** provides positive feedback to group members.

- **Go-For** leaves his or her seat to get materials and equipment for the group, and runs group errands to perform tasks such as sharpening pencils.

4. What Rules Should Be Established So That Groups Can Function Independently Of The Teacher?

It is critical that a common set of guidelines be established for all groups to follow when completing their assigned collaborative tasks. Five rules suggested for this purpose are:

- **You are responsible for your own behavior in the group.**

- **You are accountable for contributing to the assigned task.**

- **You are expected to help any group member who wants help, needs help, or asks for help.**

- **You will ask the teacher for help only when everyone in the group has the same need.**

- **You may not "put down" another person in any way.**

5. What Is Meant By Social Or Processing Skills?

Cooperative learning puts as much emphasis on students' acquisition of social skills as it does on their acquisition of academic skills. Positive interdependence within a group must be nurtured. It is essential to be able to identify, apply, and evaluate such social processing skills as listening to others, taking turns, offering help, sharing resources, exchanging ideas, disagreeing with others, stating opinions, and encouraging group members. It is possible to teach students the behaviors most commonly associated with each of these processing skills. Learning occurs most readily when concentration is put on one or two skills at a time (note the SUGGESTED SOCIAL SKILLS for each unit).

6. How Do You Evaluate Or Grade The Work Of Group Members?

It is important that group accountability and individual accountability become part of the cooperative learning task. Group accountability occurs when a co-produced end product earns a group grade, a co-performed demonstration earns a group reward, or a group test earns a group letter rating. Another way to encourage group accountability is to administer individual written tests to the group members, then to select one paper at random to assess as representative of the group's understanding (this also encourages individual accountability). The individual student may also be held accountable when written tests or individual projects are graded individually.

7. What Are The Steps To Follow When Setting Up A Cooperative Learning Group Activity In The Classroom?

Follow this procedure when establishing cooperative learning tasks for a group of students:

1. Decide on the group task or goal. Write out directions and guidelines for students to use.

2. Decide on the size of the group and assign group members. Make certain the group's size and makeup are appropriate for its mission.

3. Assign roles to group members. Make certain that everyone has a specific job to perform.

4. Determine which social processing skill(s) will be emphasized during the assigned activity. Review and/or teach common behaviors associated with the chosen skill(s).

5. Review the rules for functioning in a group setting. Discuss reasons for each rule.

6. Select a group and/or individual method for assessing the group's performance. Consider such options as observations, anecdotal records, written tests, end products, or verbal explanations/demonstrations.

8. How Often Should Cooperative Learning Groups Be Used To Deliver Classroom Instruction?

It is suggested by Johnson and Johnson that cooperative learning groups be balanced by other types of delivery systems, including those that are both individualized and competitive in nature (1987). These authors recommend that approximately one third of class time be used for formalized cooperative learning strategies.

9. Are There Advantages To Using Cooperative Learning To Teach Thematic Units?

Cooperative learning is based on building "linkages" or "bridges," not only among students, but among various disciplines and types of subject matter. Thematic units also "link" various disciplines, by use of a common theme. Using cooperative learning strategies to teach thematic units is a powerful method for demonstrating to students the advantages of "pooling" human talents and interests, the advantages of being able to see the inter-relationships among fields of study, and the advantages of drawing from various fields of study when engaged in learning enterprises—all excellent preparation for the work of the future.

10. Why Is There A Logical Connection Between Whole Language, Thematic Units, And Cooperative Learning?

Whole language uses reading or language arts as a focus for integrating disciplines and sharing "people power" in the classroom or school setting. In the whole language classroom, the teacher will develop thematic units that blend the content of various subject areas while relying on the interactions of students. These two educational delivery systems also overlap with cooperative learning in many ways. All three are invaluable for nurturing teamwork and connecting curriculum.

THEMATIC UNITS

Reference Skills Sharpeners • Content Mini-Units
Interdisciplinary Unit • Design-Your-Own Units

ARTIFACT ADVENTURE

Purpose:
To consider the use of artifacts as a means of communication.

Materials Needed:
- Copy of Student Worksheet for each group
- Box for collecting artifacts for each group
- Folder for each group
- Paper and pencils

Suggested Group Size:
Five

Suggested Group Roles:
Coordinator, Recorder, Reader, Encourager, and Go-For

Suggested Social Skills:
Encouraging and acknowledging individual and group contributions

Suggested Methods Of Accountability:
Individual – Demonstrated ability to use artifacts as a learning tool
Group – Quality of artifacts display and contents of group folder

Directions:
- Work with your group to complete each of the six activities.
- Place all the written work in your group folder.

Bonus Total Group Project:
　　With your small group, gather together a collection of artifacts that say something about your school. The members of your group will work together to write a short skit about the school, using the artifacts as props.

　　Each small group will present its skit to the total group. Use the democratic process to determine the best skit. Each student will vote by secret ballot for his or her favorite.

ARTIFACT ADVENTURE

KNOWLEDGE:
Come up with a group definition of "artifact."

COMPREHENSION:
Explain how artifacts can give us information about a particular time or place or about the habits/lifestyle of a group of people.

APPLICATION:
Over a period of one day, collect artifacts that represent our "throw-away" culture. You may gather them from the classroom and around the school, and even bring a few from home. Use them to make an informative display.

ANALYSIS:
Draw conclusions about what could be done to promote the use of artifacts as a tool for learning more about ecology in the classroom or school setting.

SYNTHESIS:
Write a short science fiction story about a group of scientists in the year 3000 A.D. who dig up some American artifacts from the 1990's. What would they conclude about our culture? If you prefer, your project may be put in the form of a report written by the scientists. One member of your group may do the actual writing while the others contribute ideas.

EVALUATION:
Decide what would be the ten best artifacts to represent your generation to a group of aliens from outer space. Establish criteria for making your selections.

BIOGRAPHICAL BEGINNINGS

Purpose:
To explore the biography as a reference tool for learning about important people.

Materials Needed:
- Copy of Student Worksheet for each group
- Copy of Guide For Studying the Life of a Person (page 134) for each student
- Magazines
- Media center materials for ANALYSIS Activity
- Paper and pencils

Suggested Group Size:
Two

Suggested Group Roles:
Reader and Recorder

Suggested Social Skills:
Sharing ideas and following directions

Suggested Methods Of Accountability:
Individual – Individual magazine reports
Group – Successful completion of all Bloom activities

Directions:
- With your partner, discuss and write down your combined responses to all the activities below except for the APPLICATION Activity. Put these responses in a folder.
- Work by yourself to complete the APPLICATION Activity. Have your partner check over your rough draft for errors in grammar or expression of ideas before you rewrite it in final form.
- Add both of your magazine reports to the folder for the teacher to collect.

Bonus Total Group Project:
Each pair of students will choose a V.I.P. in your school to research, i.e., the principal, librarian, custodian, secretary, P.E. teacher, etc. Use the Guide For Studying The Life Of A Person (page 134) to gather information about the life of your chosen V.I.P. Your group of two will work together to collect, compile, and edit information for the preparation of a final biography. The entire class will compile the edited and carefully-written biographies into a booklet for the reading table. Call the booklet *School V.I.P.'s*. Caricatures can be added for extra interest.

BIOGRAPHICAL BEGINNINGS

KNOWLEDGE:

Work together to agree on some famous people whose biographies you would like to read. Choose one person from each of these categories: Sports Figure, Television Star, Explorer, Author, Foreign Leader, and Inventor.

COMPREHENSION:

Put your heads together and define "biography," using your own words. Explain how a biography is different from an autobiography.

APPLICATION:

Choose a famous person who is of interest to you and do some research on him or her. Construct a simple "magazine report" by writing down 6–10 facts from your research and putting each one on a separate piece of paper. Find a magazine illustration to go with each fact and paste it on the appropriate page. Make a cover and title page for your biography booklet.

ANALYSIS:

Work together to select titles of 20 different biographies from the card catalog/microfiche in your media center. Classify these titles/biographies in some way so that you have no fewer than three categories (you may have more). Write a statement for each category telling what each title/biography has in common with the others within that group.

SYNTHESIS:

Working together, create a Name Poem for each of the biography characters from the APPLICATION activity above. Each letter in a name will provide the first letter for a word or phrase. (Write each name in vertical format, leaving space to add a word or phrase to the right of each letter.)

EVALUATION:

List three people you both know or admire that you think should have biographies written about them. Be prepared to give reasons for your choices.

CATALOG COUNTDOWN

Purpose:
To evaluate both the advantages and the limitations of using the catalog as a means of acquiring a consumer product.

Materials Needed:
- Copy of Student Worksheet for each group
- Collection of consumer mail-order catalogs
- Paper and pencils
- Crayons or colored markers for SYNTHESIS Activity

Suggested Group Size:
Four

Suggested Group Roles:
Reader, Recorder, Evaluator, Encourager

Suggested Social Skills:
Sharing materials and ideas

Suggested Methods Of Accountability:
Individual – Oral responses to EVALUATION Activity
Group – Successful completion of all Bloom tasks, and degree of consensus of opinion regarding the usefulness of mail-order catalogs for acquiring consumer products

Directions:
- Each member of your group of four will choose a catalog to complete the KNOWLEDGE task.
- The group members will then share their information and jointly complete the other five tasks.
- When finished, the teacher will ask you to turn in your group's written responses to these tasks.
- Be sure each of you can explain in your own words why the catalog is or is not a good means of acquiring consumer products.

Bonus Total Group Project:
Design and produce a catalog of school-supply items appropriate for your class. Include:
...illustrations, descriptions, catalog numbers, and prices for all items.
...full ordering information, including an appropriate order form.
...front and back covers.
Brainstorm and plan the project in a total group setting. Then work in your groups of four to complete designated tasks. Reconvene the total group to evaluate completion of small group work and to compile sections to make the catalog.
Share the completed catalog with another class or place it in the media center with a "reaction sheet" asking for feedback. You will want to know what other students think of the relevance of your product selection, presentation, and pricing.

CATALOG COUNTDOWN

KNOWLEDGE:

Select a catalog and write down three features that you like about the catalog.

COMPREHENSION:

In your small group, summarize some advantages and disadvantages of ordering products from a catalog.

APPLICATION:

Work together to develop a checklist for classmates to use in evaluating the reliability of catalog advertising.

ANALYSIS:

Pool your lists from the KNOWLEDGE activity and compare the four catalogs in terms of cover attractiveness, format, product descriptions, readability, and organization.

SYNTHESIS:

Work together to compose a catalog page that presents at least three products. Include illustrations, product descriptions, catalog item numbers, and prices.

EVALUATION:

Discuss the following question and draw conclusions: When and under what circumstances is a mail-order catalog the best means of purchasing a consumer product?

ENCYCLOPEDIA ENERGIZERS

Purpose:
To determine both the advantages and the limitations of using the encyclopedia as a reference tool.

Materials Needed:
- Copy of Student Worksheet for each group
- Sets of encyclopedias
- Paper and pencils

Suggested Group Size:
Three

Suggested Group Roles:
Reader, Checker, and Recorder

Suggested Group Social Skills:
Sharing materials and ideas

Suggested Accountability:
Individual – Oral response to Evaluation task
Group – Quality of Encyclopedia Treasure Hunt items

Directions:
- To complete the KNOWLEDGE Activity, each member of your group will choose a different encyclopedia.
- All group members will share information and jointly complete the other five tasks.
- When finished, the teacher will ask you to turn in your group's written responses to these tasks.
- Be sure each of you can tell in your own words when the encyclopedia is a good tool for you to use in the classroom, and when it is not.

Bonus Total Group Project:
Each group will be assigned a high-interest research topic by the teacher (sample topics: Endangered Plant or Animal Species, Space Exploration, Robots, History of The Olympics, The United Nations ...). Students in each group will work together, using encyclopedias to gather information which will be used to prepare a comprehensive report on the topic.

Rather than limiting yourselves to the traditional report written in paragraph form, you may create a collage or mural, cartoon strips, a diorama, or use newspaper or magazine formats for your report.

Time should be allowed for all reports to be presented to the total group. Culminate the activity with a group discussion of the availability and accuracy of the information found in the encyclopedias.

ENCYCLOPEDIA ENERGIZERS

KNOWLEDGE:
Select an encyclopedia and write down some things that you like about it. Each member of your group of three should choose a different encyclopedia.

COMPREHENSION:
Working with your small group, summarize the problems that students can have when they abuse or overuse the encyclopedia for a classroom assignment.

APPLICATION:
Together, produce an Encyclopedia Treasure Hunt for classmates to use for practicing their research skills.

ANALYSIS:
Pool your information from the KNOWLEDGE Activity and compare the three chosen encyclopedias in terms of format, organization, eye appeal, content, illustrations, print/type size, etc.

SYNTHESIS:
Make up a group magazine ad for one of the three encyclopedias from the KNOWLEDGE activity. Choose an encyclopedia that has special appeal to kids of your age.

EVALUATION:
Discuss and draw conclusions: When is an encyclopedia the best reference tool and when is it the least effective reference tool to use when completing a classroom assignment?

GUIDED LEARNING

Purpose:
To explore the multiple uses of a guide.

Materials Needed:
- Copy of Student Worksheet for each group
- Dictionaries
- Folders
- Paper and pencils
- Crayons or colored markers for SYNTHESIS Activity

Suggested Group Size:
Two

Suggested Group Roles:
Coordinator and Recorder

Suggested Social Skills:
Staying on task

Suggested Methods Of Accountability:
Individual — Personal definition of word "guide" as used in the context of these activities
Group — Quality of Guidebook and of Rating Scale from SYNTHESIS and EVALUATION Activities

Directions:
- Complete activities as directed.
- Put all finished work in a folder for your group.

Bonus Total Group Project:
Work in small groups to plan field trips on the school grounds. Each field trip should have a specific learning objective. A learning objective might be to evaluate safety measures taken with regards to entrances and exits. Other ideas: to study the condition and location of playground and P.E. equipment, to locate and identify trees and shrubs, or to determine what is needed for litter control and campus beautification. Each group should develop a guide to follow to achieve its objective.

In a total group setting, present and evaluate the guides. Using the democratic process (one person, one vote), select one field trip for the entire group to carry out.

GUIDED LEARNING

KNOWLEDGE:

Working together, record the multiple definitions in the dictionary for the word "guide." Circle the definition that is best for research and reference purposes.

COMPREHENSION:

Take turns telling each other about a time when some type of "guide" was of great help to you, or about a time when some type of "guide" would have been a lifesaver.

APPLICATION:

Select a country. Study the country of your choice, using the Guide For Studying A Country on page 136.

ANALYSIS:

Analyze your guided tour from the APPLICATION Activity and determine which parts you are most proud of and which parts you would like to leave out. Discover some reasons for having student "guides" as an important part of your school's visitation process.

SYNTHESIS:

Design a "self-touring guidebook" for your school or community. This should be a guide that will take its user from beginning to end of an interesting tour. Make the guidebook original, creative, colorful, and informative.

EVALUATION:

Establish a rating scale of some kind and use it to rate each of the places/programs on your guided tour from the APPLICATION Activity above.

MAPTIME MANDATE

Purpose:
To identify types of information to be found on a world map and to practice applying basic map skills.

Materials Needed:
- Copy of Student Worksheet for each group
- Map of the world, globe, and world atlas
- Paper and pencils

Suggested Group Size:
Four

Suggested Group Roles:
Coordinator, Recorder, Timekeeper, and Evaluator

Suggested Social Skills:
Energizing group

Suggested Methods Of Accountability:
Individual — Identification of types of information commonly found on a map (KNOWLEDGE Activity)
Group — Quality of plans for trip from APPLICATION Activity and quality of plans for Invent-A-Country from SYNTHESIS Activity

Directions:
- Complete activities according to directions given.
- Try to help one another come up with the best ideas and best products possible.

Bonus Total Group Project:
The teacher will provide a large world map, pins, and yarn, and each student will receive a copy of the World Map (page 135). A discussion leader and two recorders will be appointed.

In a total group brainstorming discussion, decide on a "dream destination" for a class visit. There are only three requirements:
1. The journey must last no longer than seven days.
2. The teacher and school principal will serve as group leaders.
3. The trip must be planned to carry out some socially beneficial objective such as world peace, cultural literacy, or environmental benefits.

When the class has agreed on a destination, the recorders will follow group directions to plot the best course for the trip, pinning and re-pinning the yarn in place on the world map. Consider availability of transportation, historic, cultural, or scenic sites to be visited en route, and other geographical concerns. Each student will also trace the route on his or her Worksheet and add items of interest as defined through group discussion.

MAPTIME MANDATE

KNOWLEDGE:
Working as a group, identify all the different types of information you can find on a world map. Try to develop an idea for each letter of the alphabet, e.g., D is for "Distances Between Cities."

COMPREHENSION:
Each person in the group will select 20 different places on a World Map and write them down. Group or categorize them in some way. Describe your classification scheme. Each member of the group should examine all the lists. Are your groupings alike or different? Try to combine lists and categorize all 80 places in some logical way.

APPLICATION:
Together, plan a ten-day trip in one country of the world. Where will you go and what will you do? How will you get there and how will you move about? What will you have to pack and what kind of money will you need?

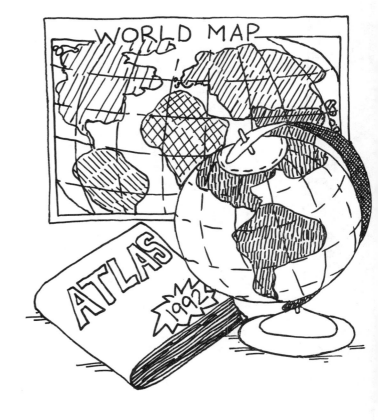

ANALYSIS:
Together, compare and contrast a world map with a globe and with an atlas. List the advantages and disadvantages of each. Tell when one might be a more effective tool to use than the other.

SYNTHESIS:
Invent a new country! Describe its size, population, location, and topography. Tell about its people, its style of life, its government, and its economy.

EVALUATION:
In your group's opinion, what should be the Eighth Wonder of the World? What criteria will you use and what defense can you give to validate your choice?

POSTER POWER

Purpose:
To explore the value of posters as learning tools in the classroom.

Materials Needed:
- Posters
- Copy of Student Worksheet for each group
- Paper and pencils

Suggested Group Size:
Two

Suggested Group Roles:
Recorder and Checker

Suggested Social Skills:
Taking turns

Suggested Methods Of Accountability:
Individual — Response from Synthesis Activity
Group — Responses from all other Activities

Directions:
- Complete each of the suggested tasks with your partner except for the Synthesis Activity.
- Complete the Synthesis Activity individually. Take time to critique each other's work before turning it in.

Bonus Total Group Project:
Work together with a partner to design an original poster to promote environmental concerns. Use one of the following themes:

Save Our Trees   Let's Clean Up Our Act
Re-use, Recycle, Or Refuse Don't Litter—It Hurts
Don't Pollute Our Streams   Save The Planet Earth

Display the completed posters and use the criteria developed in the EVALUATION Activity to select a poster for each of the following categories:

The Most Original Poster
The Poster That Best Communicates Its Message
The Best Poster Over All

POSTER POWER

KNOWLEDGE:

Select a poster and answer the following questions about it using a series of complete sentences:
Who or what is the poster about?
What is its setting or background?
Why is it a good or a poor poster?
How does it convey information?

COMPREHENSION:

In your own words, tell why some posters are considered forms of communication rather than art forms.

APPLICATION:

Construct a series of questions to ask other students about the poster selected for the KNOWLEDGE Activity. The questions should require skill or interpretation to answer. One question might be, "What are ten descriptive words you could use to tell about the poster?"

ANALYSIS:

Determine what you might do to improve the quality or message of this poster.

SYNTHESIS:

Use the poster as a springboard for writing any two of the following types of poetry: Haiku, Limerick, Free Verse, Diamante, Tanka, or Concrete.

EVALUATION:

Establish a set of criteria for judging the quality of a poster. Use the criteria to assign a grade to the poster selected for the Knowledge Activity.

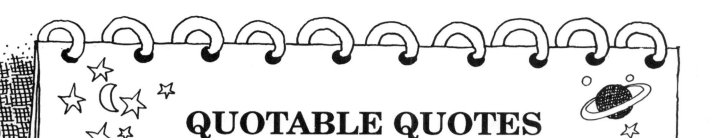

QUOTABLE QUOTES

Purpose:
To develop an appreciation for the well-known sayings of famous people.

Materials Needed:
- Copy of Student Worksheet for each group
- Copy of *Bartlett's Familiar Quotations*
- Paper and pencils

Suggested Group Size:
Two

Suggested Group Roles:
Recorder and Timekeeper

Suggested Social Skills:
Discussion and cooperative decision-making

Suggested Methods Of Accountability:
Individual — Ability to describe *Bartlett's Familiar Quotations* as a reference tool after completing COMPREHENSION Activity, and quality of illustration from SYNTHESIS Activity
Group — Quality of quotation comparison from ANALYSIS Activity

Directions:
- Complete all activities as directed.
- Be prepared to tell the teacher how *Bartlett's Familiar Quotations* can be regarded as a reference tool for student use.

Bonus Total Group Project:
Work together as a total group to make your own Book of Quotations (proverbs, funny sayings, mottos, serious thoughts) by interviewing people that you know. First meet as a total group and set your plan of action by determining whom you will interview to gather your quotations, how many quotations each student will be responsible for, and what the format of your book will be.

When you interview a person, ask for a saying or "quotation" that has been meaningful during his or her life. Try to copy it down as accurately as possible, and try to determine a source. The source may be a relative, friend, famous person, "Anonymous," or even "Unknown."

Reconvene as a large group with your pages of quotations. Designate small groups to come up with an interesting title, to design a cover, to copy quotations if necessary, to arrange the pages, and to bind the book. Put it on the reading table for all to enjoy.

QUOTABLE QUOTES

KNOWLEDGE:
Working with your partner, copy down five quotations from *Bartlett's Familiar Quotations* that both of you like very much.

COMPREHENSION:
Discuss and describe ways the two of you might use *Bartlett's Familiar Quotations* as a learning tool.

APPLICATION:
Take turns relating a personal incident that illustrates the meaning of one of the quotations from the KNOWLEDGE Activity.

"Money doesn't grow on trees."

ANALYSIS:
Together, compare and contrast two different quotations on the same topic. Sample topics: success, money, parents, school, death.

SYNTHESIS:
Produce a picture to illustrate a quotation of your choice.

EVALUATION:
Criticize the following statement as you think Bartlett might: "A picture is worth a thousand words."

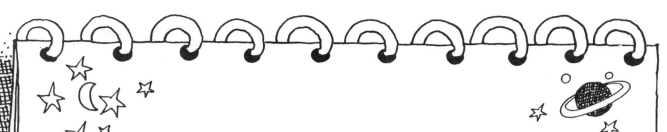

MASTERING MYSTERIES

Purpose:
To consider the appeal and elements of the mystery story.

Materials Needed:
Paper and pencils

Suggested Group Roles:
Coordinator, Recorder, and Checker

Suggested Group Size:
Three

Suggested Social Skills:
Responding to ideas of others and group planning

Suggested Methods Of Accountability:
Individual — Individual detective story chapter
Group — Successful completion of all group activities and group feedback on original stories

Directions:
• Work together to complete each of the activities on the Mastering Mysteries Activity Sheet.

MASTERING MYSTERIES

Learning Activities

1. List at least ten television, movie, or fictional detective characters.

2. Write definitions for the following terms in your own words:
   - detective
   - mystery
   - villain
   - witness
   - clue
   - sleuth
   - suspect
   - innocent bystander

3. Working as a group, recommend a favorite detective (from comic strips, well-known television programs, movies, or fiction) for a Mystery Hall of Fame. Give reasons for your choice.

4. Write a short three-chapter detective story. Each member of your group should contribute one chapter. Together, outline your plot, characters, and setting. Organize the ideas so that the chapters provide an orderly sequence of events.

5. Illustrate the completed story.

6. Place your completed work on the reading table for the entire group to enjoy.

OCEAN OUTREACH

Purpose:
To learn about the ocean, ocean life, and ocean-related careers.

Materials Needed:
- Copy of Student Worksheet for each group
- Reference books containing material on ocean subjects
- Paper and pencils

Suggested Group Size:
Three

Suggested Group Roles:
Coordinator, Timekeeper, and Recorder

Suggested Social Skills:
Pooling ideas, concepts, and skills to complete specific learning tasks.

Suggested Methods Of Accountability:
Individual — Student will be able to knowledgeably answer questions related to features and characteristics of the ocean
Group — Satisfactory completion of all activities and quality of feedback during total group discussion

Directions:
- Work with your group members to complete all of the activities on the Learning Activities Worksheet.

OCEAN OUTREACH

Learning Activities

1. Use the dictionary and reference books to define each of the following words or terms:

   ocean
   oceanography
   tides
   ecosystems
   seas

2. Differentiate between an ocean and a sea. List two characteristics of each.

3. Write a resumé for a person applying for one of the following ocean-related careers (give specific education, job experience, and talents that might help to qualify the person for the job):

   Marine Biologist
   Deep-Sea Diver
   Commercial Fisherman
   Oceanographer

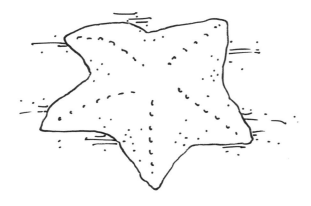

4. Study the physical characteristics, habits, habitats, and other features of five sea animals. Select two of the five and compare their expected life spans and the dangers they are subject to in their ocean lives.

5. Make up four math word problems with ocean-related themes. Write each problem on one index card and each answer on another one (you will have eight cards in all). Place your problems and answers in a designated spot for classmates to "mix and match."

RAINBOWS
AND
RAINDROPS

Purpose:
To learn about the elements of precipitation.

Materials Needed:
- Paper and pencils
- Watercolor painting materials

Suggested Group Size:
Four

Suggested Group Roles:
Coordinator, Recorder, Go-For, and Praiser

Suggested Social Skills:
Responding to ideas of others and group planning

Suggested Methods Of Accountability:
Individual — Ability to define and explain at least three different forms of precipitation
Group — Satisfactory completion of all group activities and total group feedback related to art projects

Directions:
- Decide who will complete each of the activities on the Rainbows and Raindrops Activity Sheet, and work together to help one another to complete the assigned tasks.

Cooperative Learning Guide for Middle Grades- Incentive

RAINBOWS AND RAINDROPS

Learning Activities

1. List three major types of precipitation. Briefly explain how each is formed.

2. Suggest at least five ways that animals and people benefit from rain.

3. Predict the conditions that must exist in order for a rainbow to occur. Tell how a prism can be used to create a rainbow.

4. Use weather words to create a crossword or wordfinder puzzle.

5. Decide if your group is more like...
   - . . . raindrop or rainbow.
   - . . . lightning bolt or thunderbolt.
   - . . . hazy day or sunny day.
   - . . . drought or drizzle.
   - . . . cumulonimbus or cirrostratus cloud.

   Give reasons for each answer.

6. Use watercolors, chalk, or felt tip pens to create a group picture of a rainbow. Remember to use all five colors of the rainbow. Write a poem or song to accompany your picture.

7. Display completed art projects and ask for reactions from the total group.

VENN DIAGRAMS

Purpose:
To demonstrate the use of Venn diagrams in mathematics.

Materials Needed:
- Copy of Student Worksheet for each group
- Mathematics book that contains information on Venn diagrams
- Paper and pencils

Suggested Group Size:
Two

Suggested Group Roles:
Recorder and Timekeeper

Suggested Social Skills:
Offering and accepting help to complete specific learning tasks

Suggested Methods Of Accountability:
Individual — Satisfactory completion of all tasks
Group — Satisfactory completion of all tasks and quality of original Venn diagrams

Directions:
- Work with your partner to complete activities on Activity Sheet.

VENN DIAGRAMS

Learning Activities

1. Use the glossary and index of a math book to define "Venn diagram" and give an example of one.

2. Explain how Venn diagrams are helpful in showing mathematical relationships.

3. Give several examples of other graphic forms that show relationships between or among objects. Consider examples used in language arts, social studies, and science.

4. Draw a series of Venn diagrams to show the relationship of numbers in some unusual or creative way.

5. Share your completed diagrams with the total group.

CALENDAR CAPERS

Purpose:
To explore the calendar as an organizational tool and to gain information about the history and the economic and social significance of calendars through the ages.

Materials Needed:
- Collection of calendars
- Copy of Thought-A-Day Calendar (page 137) for each group
- Reference books
- Colored markers
- Paper and pencils

Suggested Group Size:
Four

Suggested Group Roles:
Coordinator, Recorder, and Checkers

Suggested Social Skills:
Planning, problem-solving, and sharing

Suggested Methods Of Accountability:
Individual – Ability to demonstrate knowledge of the history and use of calendars in society and to make meaningful use of a personal calendar
Group – Quality of Thought-A-Day Calendar (see Culminating Activity).

Directions:
- Initiate the unit and build readiness for the learning activities by presenting the Motivational Activity.
- Complete Learning Activities as directed.
- Follow procedure for Culminating Activity. Enjoy the completed calendars!

Motivational Activity:
Ask students to bring various kinds of calendars to school. (Provide some of your own calendars to ensure a wide variety.) Present the calendars in a total group setting and pass them around for students to examine. Lead a discussion based on the different types of calendars and their intended use. Discuss sizes, illustrations, type styles, formats, quality of paper, prices, and special features.

To encourage lively participation, present discussion sparkers such as the following:
- What is the most important day, month, or week of the year? Why?
- What would happen if a worldwide ban was imposed on the use of calendars for a full year?
- How would your life be affected if the calendar year was one month longer (13 months instead of 12)?

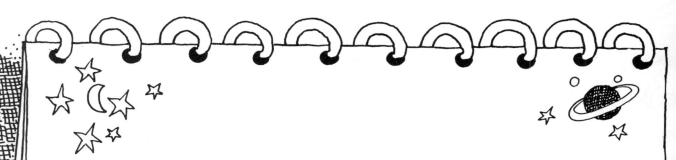

Use the democratic process to select calendars from the collection for each of the following awards:

Most Attractive Calendar
Best-Illustrated Calendar
Most Useful Calendar For Students
"Tackiest" Calendar
Funniest Calendar

Stage the "election" by having nominators hold up calendars for each category and support their choices with speeches not more than five sentences in length. Ask students to "vote" by clapping their hands. The calendar receiving the heaviest applause in each category will be declared the winner.

Display the winners with appropriate labels on a bulletin board.

Culminating Activity:

Reproduce and distribute copies of the calendar sheet on page 137 to each small group. Ask each group to plan a Thought-A-Day Calendar for the next month, listing something for each day. Suggest the inclusion of:

A Famous Person's Birthday
Riddles and Jokes
Special Activities
Historical Events

Display completed calendars on a bulletin board or reading table for the entire group to peruse and discuss.

Learning Activity I:

KNOWLEDGE

1. Write down as many words that begin with cal_____ as you can brainstorm in 3 minutes.

2. What are some items people most commonly write on their calendars? List at least 10 items.

3. Define the word "calendar." Use reference books to locate the following information: Who designed the first calendar? When? Why? Where? Brainstorm and write a short story related to your findings.

Group Plan: _____

_____

_____

_____

_____

_____

Summary and Evaluation: _____

_____

_____

_____

_____

_____

Learning Activity II:

COMPREHENSION

1. Extend each of these sentence starters:

   A calendar is especially useful when . . .
   A calendar makes a nice gift because . . .
   An outdated calendar can be used to . . .
   The busiest month on the school cal-
       endar is _____ because . . .

2. Write a paragraph or design a comic
   strip to show why one person may need
   to use two or more calendars on a daily
   basis.

3. Make a poster that shows examples of
   various types of calendars. Summarize
   the components of each calendar on
   your poster.

Group Plan: _____

_____

_____

_____

_____

Summary and Evaluation: _____

_____

_____

_____

_____

Learning Activity III:

APPLICATION

1. Use the following symbols to mark a calendar for the next five days. Write a weather report for each day, and a forecast for the following day.

   Sunshine   *Cloudy*   *Rain*   *Snow*   *Storm*

2. Schools often distribute school calendars at the beginning of the school year. These calendars usually list dates and activities planned for each date. Develop a more extensive format for your school to use when preparing the year's calendar. Now, organize a presentation to help you sell your calendar idea to your principal.

3. The Girl Scout organization has sold calendars for many years. Write a list of questions to ask the Girl Scouts of America about their annual calendar sales. Combine your questions with the questions listed by other groups. Write a class letter to the Girl Scout Headquarters in your area to get the answers to your questions.

Group Plan: _____

_____

_____

_____

_____

Summary and Evaluation: _____

_____

_____

_____

Learning Activity IV:

ANALYSIS

1. Infer the types of daily events you might find listed on the personal calendars of the following people:

   The Chief Of Police
   The President
   A Movie Star
   A Professional Football Player
   Mickey Mouse
   A Pop Singer

2. Make a chart that compares the Gregorian, Islamic, and Hebrew calendars.

3. Compare and contrast the purpose of an everyday household calendar with that of a daily journal.

Group Plan: _____

_____

_____

_____

_____

_____

Summary and Evaluation: _____

_____

_____

_____

_____

_____

Learning Activity V:

SYNTHESIS

1. Predict all the possible effects of a secretary's having lost the boss's appointment calendar.

2. Will we have calendars in the year 2000? Design a new calendar format. Describe and draw the calendar. Tell how it differs from any other calendar presently on the market.

3. You have been chosen to select the Calendar of the Year. Develop the criteria you would use in your selection process.

Group Plan: _____

_____

_____

_____

_____

_____

Summary and Evaluation: _____

_____

_____

_____

_____

Learning Activity VI:

EVALUATION

1. Determine all of the reasons you think people buy calendars. Rank order them from the most popular to the least popular.

   Now, interview several people. Find out their reasons for purchasing a calendar. Record your findings on a graph.

2. Consider whether you think the following statement is true or false: "People who use calendars are more organized than people who do not." Back up your decision with facts and examples.

3. Imagine yourself in another period of time. What types of notes would you have written on your calendar for the month of December? Justify to someone your selection of notes.

Group Plan: _____

_____

_____

_____

_____

_____

Summary and Evaluation: _____

_____

_____

_____

_____

_____

☆ ☽ ☆ FOSTERING FIRST AID

Purpose:
To list and explain the contents of a typical first-aid kit.

Materials Needed:
- First-aid kits
- Paper and pencils

Suggested Group Size:
Four

Suggested Group Roles:
Coordinator, Reader, Recorder, and Go-For

Suggested Social Skills:
Planning, and offering and accepting help to complete specific tasks

Suggested Methods Of Accountability:

Individual – Ability to describe types and purposes of items in a first-aid kit

Group – Successful completion of at least one activity at each level of Bloom's Taxonomy

Directions:
TO BE DETERMINED BY TEACHER AND GROUP (include Motivational and Culminating Activities):

_____

_____

_____

_____

_____

_____

_____

_____

_____

_____

_____

_____

Learning Activity I:

KNOWLEDGE

1. State the most important purpose of a first-aid kit.

2. Write down the ten items most likely to be found in a standard first-aid kit.

3. Record all the places where a first-aid kit should be located.

Group Plan: _____

_____

_____

_____

_____

_____

Summary and Evaluation: _____

_____

_____

_____

_____

_____

Learning Activity II:

COMPREHENSION

1. Describe the proper procedure for each of the following medical emergencies:

   a. Reviving someone who feels faint or has fainted.
   b. Cleansing a wound or cut.
   c. Treating a person for shock.

2. Arrange the ten items most likely to be found in a first-aid kit in alphabetical order.

3. Give examples of occasions when you might use each of the ten items in a typical first-aid kit.

Group Plan: _____

_____

_____

_____

_____

_____

Summary and Evaluation: _____

_____

_____

_____

_____

Learning Activity III:

APPLICATION

1. Show the proper procedure for the Heimlich Maneuver.

2. Demonstrate the way to properly administer CPR.

3. Practice applying a tourniquet to someone's arm or leg.

Group Plan: _____

_____

_____

_____

_____

_____

Summary and Evaluation: _____

_____

_____

_____

_____

_____

_____

Learning Activity IV:

ANALYSIS

1. Examine a first-aid kit and classify each of the items in some way.

2. Make an outline of the contents of a good first-aid course for kids.

3. Describe the type of person you think is most likely to become a health care worker.

Group Plan: _____

_____

_____

_____

_____

_____

Summary and Evaluation: _____

_____

_____

_____

_____

_____

Learning Activity V:

SYNTHESIS

1. Create a skit to show the importance of requiring prospective parents to know basic first-aid procedures before they have children.

2. Design a first-aid kit of the future. Invent the wondrous tools it might contain.

3. Devise a series of cartoons that depict the right and wrong ways to apply first aid.

Group Plan: _____

_____

_____

_____

_____

_____

_____

Summary and Evaluation: _____

_____

_____

_____

_____

_____

Learning Activity VI:

EVALUATION

1. Develop a first-aid quiz and give it to three different people. Use the results to determine what could to be done to improve the first-aid I.Q. of others.

2. Recommend three ways that first-aid classes can be effectively delivered to the public.

3. Judge the quality of a first-aid kit at home or at school. What criteria will you use to make your assessment?

Group Plan: _____

_____

_____

_____

_____

_____

Summary and Evaluation: _____

_____

_____

_____

_____

_____

GAINING MEASUREMENT MOMENTUM

Purpose:
To investigate the world of measurement and its influence on daily life.

Materials Needed:
- Reference books
- Paper and pencils
- Materials needed for Motivational and Culminating Activities

Suggested Group Size:
Three or Four

Suggested Group Roles:
Coordinator, Recorder and Checker

Suggested Social Skills:
Pooling ideas and resources to solve problems and verify answers

Suggested Methods Of Accountability:
Individual and Group – Successful completion of at least one activity for each level of Bloom's Taxonomy

Directions:
TO BE DETERMINED BY TEACHER AND GROUP (include Motivational and Culminating Activities):

_____

_____

_____

_____

_____

_____

_____

_____

_____

Learning Activity I:

KNOWLEDGE

1. List as many things as you can think of that a person cannot measure.

2. Name a measurement device. Identify at least three ways in which this device is used to make our lives easier.

3. Brainstorm a list of objects around which you could tie a one-meter string.

Group Plan: _____

_____

_____

_____

_____

_____

Summary and Evaluation: _____

_____

_____

_____

_____

Learning Activity II:

COMPREHENSION

1. Give some examples of occupations that require frequent use of standard measurement devices. Show your occupation examples and devices in chart form.

2. Prepare a list of expressions or song titles that refer to measurement in some way.

3. Explain the function of a non-standard measurement device.

Group Plan: _____

_____

_____

_____

_____

Summary and Evaluation: _____

_____

_____

_____

_____

Learning Activity III:

APPLICATION

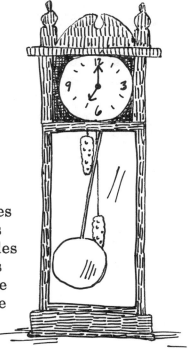

1. Look up the many different measurement systems we use or have used in the past. Write a short paragraph about each one of them.

2. Make an outline that shows how you would schedule and run a measurement tournament or contest for your school.

3. Create a logical drawing, using only lines and circles as specified. In other words, you will use 10 five-centimeter lines in your drawing, 6 one-centimeter lines, etc. You may use the lines and circles in any combination, but do not add any other lines or shapes.

   10 five-centimeter lines
   6 one-centimeter lines
   2 four-centimeter circles
   4 two-centimeter lines
   1 three-centimeter line
   1 five-centimeter circle

Group Plan: _____

_____

_____

_____

_____

Summary and Evaluation: _____

_____

_____

_____

_____

Learning Activity IV:

ANALYSIS

1. Determine why mathematics can be considered a language.

2. Do you think a partially-filled glass is half full or half empty? Explain your answer.

3. Of all the measurement devices people commonly use, which one is most likely to be used by: a teacher; an architect; a mother; a dieter; a student; a builder? Give reasons for your choices.

Group Plan: _____

_____

_____

_____

_____

Summary and Evaluation: _____

_____

_____

_____

_____

Learning Activity V:

SYNTHESIS

1. Pretend you must invent a measurement system that would measure one of the following things: Love, Fatigue, Ugliness, Truthfulness, Success, Wealth. Write about the system you would invent.

2. Develop a new measuring device. Predict the length of objects in your classroom. Test your predictions, using your new measuring device.

3. Design a ruler or meterstick that has uses other than to measure objects. Draw what it would look like and tell about the kinds of things besides measuring that could be done with the ruler.

Group Plan: _____

_____

_____

_____

_____

_____

Summary and Evaluation: _____

_____

_____

_____

_____

_____

Learning Activity VI:

EVALUATION

1. Determine all the reasons you think someone invented the metric system. Rank them in order from the most important to the least important.

2. Decide on the five most important measurement skills that every person should have. Justify your choices.

3. Defend this idea: "The measure of a man's true worth is what he would do if he knew he would never be found out."

Group Plan: _____

_____

_____

_____

_____

_____

Summary and Evaluation: _____

_____

_____

_____

_____

_____

THEMATIC THINKING SKILLS PROJECTS

Think Tank Teasers
Theme-At-A-Glance Worksheets

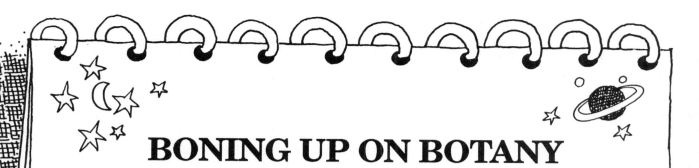

BONING UP ON BOTANY

Teacher Talk

Purpose:
To recognize the importance of plants in our environment.

Materials Needed:
- Copy of Facts To Review sheet for each group
- Copy of Activity page for each group
- Paper and pencils

Suggested Group Size:
Four

Suggested Group Roles:
Coordinator, Recorder, Reader, and Checker

Suggested Social Skills:
Speaking and listening, and developing respect for differing opinions

Suggested Methods Of Accountability:
Individual — Ability to explain the importance of plants in our environment
Group — Satisfactory completion of all activities

Directions:
- You will be teaching one another about plants by brainstorming and completing the activities as a group.
- To stimulate creative thinking, first read the information on the Facts To Review sheet.

BONING UP ON BOTANY

Facts To Review

1. Botany is the science or study of plants. A botanist examines plants—how they are structured and how they function.

2. Every plant is a living laboratory in which chemical reactions take place. Heat and light often stimulate these chemical reactions.

3. Early physicians used plants as remedies for their patients. They had to know how to distinguish between useful and poisonous plants.

4. Explorers sailing to new parts of the world found many unknown plant species. The resulting growth in demand for plant products (such as foods, fibers, drugs, and dyes) led to an increase in trade.

5. The study of plants is important to humans because most of our food comes from plants. Through the science of botany, humans can improve these vital food sources.

BONING UP ON BOTANY

Activities

1. Imagine a world without plants. List ten ways in which life would be different in such a world.

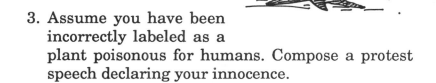

2. Pretend you are a plant suffering from too much light or heat. Describe how you feel and what is happening to you.

3. Assume you have been incorrectly labeled as a plant poisonous for humans. Compose a protest speech declaring your innocence.

4. Write a series of diary entries as if you were an explorer who has just discovered a miracle plant. What is your name? Where were you found? Who discovered you? Why are you important?

5. Create a lunch or dinner menu, including many of your favorite "plants." Describe your dishes in mouth-watering terms.

FACING UP TO FAIRY TALES

Teacher Talk

Purpose:
To explore and develop appreciation of fairy tales.

Materials Needed:
- Copy of Facts To Review sheet for each group
- Copy of Activities page for each group
- Paper, pencils, and crayons or markers for writing and art projects
- Tape recorder and tapes if Activity No. 4 is possible

Suggested Group Size:
Four

Suggested Group Roles:
Coordinator, Recorder, Checker, and Encourager

Suggested Social Skills:
Processing and using information and making group choices

Suggested Methods Of Accountability:
Individual — Quality of birthday card
Group — Quality of group portfolio of completed activities.

Directions:
- Read the facts about fairy tales on the Facts To Review sheet and discuss with the members of your group.
- Make a birthday card for the fairy tale character of your choice, following the directions on the Activity Page. Share and discuss the completed cards.
- Read and discuss the remaining Facing Up To Fairy Tales Activities and select one to complete as a group project.

FACING UP TO FAIRY TALES

Facts To Review

1. A fairy tale is a fictitious or make-believe story.

2. It is not the presence of a fairy in a story that makes it a "fairy tale." There are probably more fairy tales without fairies than there are with fairies.

3. Many of the fairy tales we know today are so old that we have no idea who made them up or who first wrote them down.

4. We do know that the first collection of European traditional stories was written by a Frenchman, Charles Perrault, in 1967. He wrote the stories for his own children. Among them were such classics as "Puss In Boots" and "Bluebeard."

5. The Brothers Grimm were two German collectors of fairy tales who tried to record stories exactly as they were told in the early 1800's. Among their most famous tales are "Hansel and Gretel" and "Tom Thumb."

6. Fairy tales have originated in almost every major culture. The Arabian Nights is a compilation of old folk and fairy tales from Asia and North Africa. Two of the most famous tales in this collection are "Aladdin and the Magic Lamp" and "Sinbad the Sailor."

FACING UP TO FAIRY TALES

Activities

1. Design a birthday card for your favorite fairy tale character. Create a rhyming verse for your card. Decorate your card and display it in the room.

2. Choose a tale in which a number is significant, such as "The Three Little Pigs" or "Sleeping Beauty." Rewrite the story using a different number. Changing the story this way should result in a different ending.

3. Write an updated version of a popular fairy tale, placing it in the 21st century. For example, the Three Little Pigs may have houses made of steel, glass, and cement block; the Three Billy Goats Gruff may try to make their way across a suspension bridge; Little Red Riding Hood may live in New York City.

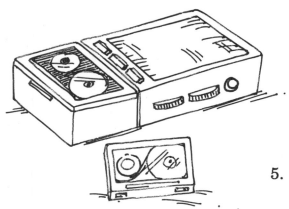

4. Tape record a fairy tale from another country. As an introduction to your story, relate 5 to 10 facts about the country in which the story originated.

5. Plan and create a collage, mural, or diorama to portray your group's favorite fairy tale.

MASTERING METRICS

Teacher Talk

Purpose:
To study selected units in the metric system.

Materials Needed:
- Copy of Facts To Review sheet for each group
- Copy of Activity page for each group
- Paper and pencils

Suggested Group Size:
Four

Suggested Group Roles:
Coordinator, Recorder, Checker, and Timekeeper

Suggested Social Skills:
Sharing ideas with others

Suggested Methods Of Accountability:
Individual — Ability to work simple math word problems that deal with grams or kilograms
Group — Satisfactory completion of all activities

Directions:
- You will be doing some fun things with the metric system. You will practice solving mathematics word problems that deal with grams and kilograms.
- Review the metric facts with one another before you begin.

MASTERING METRICS

Facts To Review

1. Scientists measure lengths, distances, weights, and other values by a method referred to as the **metric system**. The other most-commonly-used measurement system is called the **English** or the **standard** system.

2. The prefixes **deci-**, **centi-**, and **milli-** are added to base units in the metric system.

3. The metric system is based on units of 10. The principal unit of length is the **meter**, which is roughly equivalent to the standard unit **yard.**

4. The **gram** is the metric unit of weight, as is the **pound** in the standard system. One kilogram weights 1000 grams.

5. The **liter** is the basic metric unit of capacity, as is the **quart** in the standard system. One liter contains one cubic decimeter of water and weighs one kilogram.

6. A commission of French scientists developed the metric system in the 18th century. It has been revised several times. In 1960, the present form was adopted and named the International System of Units, known as SI.

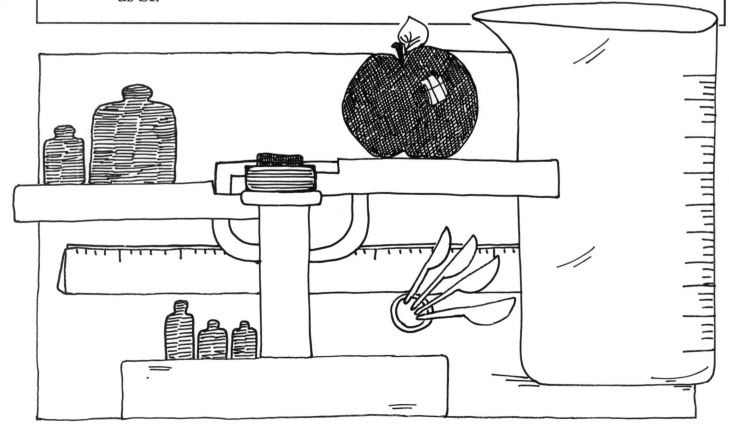

MASTERING METRICS

Activities

1. Create a folktale whose main character is one decimeter tall.

2. Pretend you are the unit Yard and write a protest speech against your counterpart, Meter.

3. Create a radio or magazine advertisement for liter containers of your group's favorite soda. Be inventive.

4. Create a series of word problems in math that deal with grams and kilograms.

5. Write a "numbers autobiography" for your group, using metric numbers. Include heights, weights, shoe sizes, favorite radio stations, addresses, etc.

TAKING A NEW LOOK
AT KITES

Teacher Talk

Purpose:
To explore the art and science of flying kites.

Materials Needed:
- Copy of Facts To Review sheet for each group
- Copy of Activity page for each group
- Paper and pencils
- Colored markers

Suggested Group Size:
Four

Suggested Group Roles:
Coordinator, Recorder, Go-For, and Encourager

Suggested Social Skills:
Encouraging individual contributions

Suggested Methods Of Accountability:
Individual — Contribution to School Kite Day
Group — Portfolio of Activity results

Directions:
- The members of your small group will all work together to complete each of the activities.
- It is important that each person in the group assume a major task in the planning and implementation of Kite Day for the class.

TAKING A NEW LOOK AT KITES

Facts To Review

1. Flying kites has been popular in Asia since 1000 B.C. Kites held great religious significance for the Chinese, Japanese, Koreans, and Malayans. Kites were believed to keep away evil spirits when flown at night.

2. Flying kites for fun has many supporters in China, where the ninth day of the ninth month is designated "Kite Day."

3. Kites have been used by people building bridges, who attached cables to kites and flew them across the river or gap.

4. Meteorologists have used kites to carry weather-recording instruments aloft.

5. A kite-flying record of note was achieved when a string of 10 kites more than nine miles long was flown successfully. The total surface of the 10 kites was 683 square feet.

6. Wilbur and Orville Wright used box kites in their early aviation experiments. What they learned about wing warping from observing kites aided them in the invention of the airplane.

TAKING A NEW LOOK AT KITES

Activities

1. Imagine what a kite might say to each of the following objects: a bird, an airplane, a tree, a child, the wind. Put your answers in comic book style, with the conversations in "balloons."

2. Plan a series of special activities and events for a school Kite Day.

3. Draw a unique kite design.

4. From the Facts to Review Sheet, you learned that kites have been used in bridge-building, meteorology, and aviation experimentation. Create a new scientific use for the kite.

5. Develop a brochure that shows the art and science of flying a kite.

AUSTRALIA

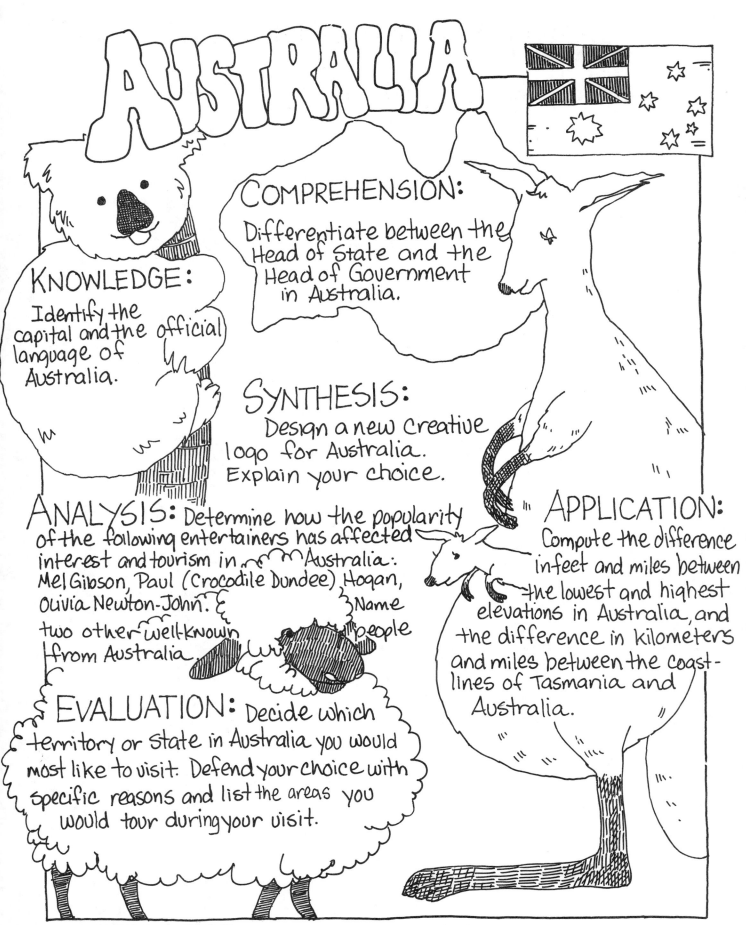

KNOWLEDGE: Identify the capital and the official language of Australia.

COMPREHENSION: Differentiate between the Head of State and the Head of Government in Australia.

SYNTHESIS: Design a new creative logo for Australia. Explain your choice.

ANALYSIS: Determine how the popularity of the following entertainers has affected interest and tourism in Australia: Mel Gibson, Paul (Crocodile Dundee) Hogan, Olivia Newton-John. Name two other well-known people from Australia.

APPLICATION: Compute the difference in feet and miles between the lowest and highest elevations in Australia, and the difference in kilometers and miles between the coastlines of Tasmania and Australia.

EVALUATION: Decide which territory or state in Australia you would most like to visit. Defend your choice with specific reasons and list the areas you would tour during your visit.

CANADA

KNOWLEDGE: Locate Canada on a world map. Name the capital and the largest city. Locate and name the countries that border Canada.

COMPREHENSION: Give examples of major Canadian imports and exports, industries, and natural resources.

APPLICATION: Classify the provinces according to size and population. Draw and cut out all the provinces and use the cutouts to make a Canadian jigsaw puzzle for study.

SYNTHESIS: Design a travel brochure that would attract visitors to Canada. Be sure to include scenic, cultural, and recreational sites.

ANALYSIS: Compare the economy, climate, and government of Canada with that of the United States. Now make the same comparisons of Canada and Mexico!

EVALUATION: Rail transportation has played a part in Canada's early history and present-day economy. Evaluate the influence of the following: early settlement, import and export traffic, industry, use of natural resources, and tourism.

CONTINENTS

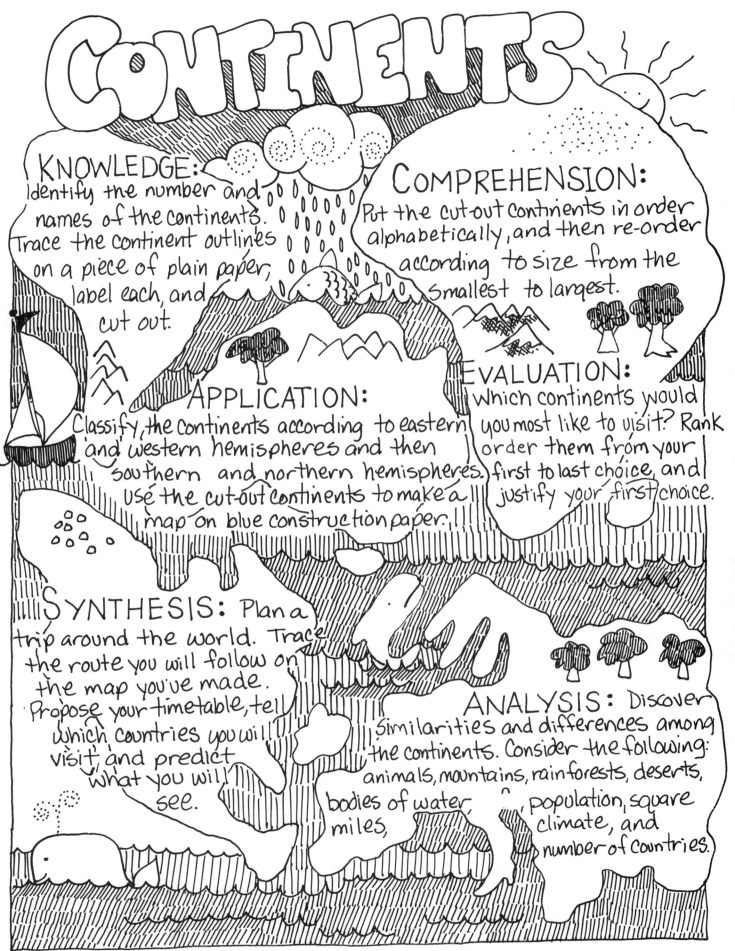

KNOWLEDGE: Identify the number and names of the continents. Trace the continent outlines on a piece of plain paper, label each, and cut out.

COMPREHENSION: Put the cut-out continents in order alphabetically, and then re-order according to size from the smallest to largest.

APPLICATION: Classify the continents according to eastern and western hemispheres and then southern and northern hemispheres. Use the cut-out continents to make a map on blue construction paper.

EVALUATION: Which continents would you most like to visit? Rank order them from your first to last choice, and justify your first choice.

SYNTHESIS: Plan a trip around the world. Trace the route you will follow on the map you've made. Propose your timetable, tell which countries you will visit, and predict what you will see.

ANALYSIS: Discover similarities and differences among the continents. Consider the following: animals, mountains, rainforests, deserts, bodies of water, population, square miles, climate, and number of countries.

GLACIERS

KNOWLEDGE: Define glacier. Distinguish between the two types of glaciers. On a world map, locate the area(s) where the majority of each type is found.

COMPREHENSION: Explain how glaciers are formed, how they move, and how they shape the land. Differentiate between a glacier and an iceberg.

APPLICATION: Construct a model of one kind of glacier, using styrofoam, clay, or a flour-salt-water mixture. Identify and label all parts.

ANALYSIS: Differentiate among the following landforms created by glaciers: lake of melted water, kettle lake, esker, bedrock, terminal moraine, cirque, fiord and drumlin.

SYNTHESIS: Glacier National Park in Montana was named for its more than fifty glaciers. Design a travel brochure to attract visitors to this national park.

EVALUATION: Glaciers greatly altered the surface of large parts of Europe and North America during the Pleistocene Ice Age, which ended 10-15,000 years ago. Consider today's warming trend: what effects might it have on the land, animals, plants, and our current way of life? Explain your answer.

JAPAN

KNOWLEDGE: Locate Japan on a world map. Count the main islands which make up this country. Name the capital of Japan and identify its latitude and longitude.

COMPREHENSION: Give examples of major Japanese imports and exports.

APPLICATION: Construct a relief map of Japan. Locate the capital and major cities. Be sure to include a key. Display.

SYNTHESIS: Design a new Japanese flag to reflect both its history and its eastern and western cultures. Color and display.

ANALYSIS: Examine the use of ceremony in traditional Japanese life & try to determine the purposes it serves.

EVALUATION: Consider how each of the following would respond to winning a ten-day, all expense-paid trip to Japan:

Geography teacher
World War II veteran
Computer salesman
A Japanese-American
President of Ford Motor Co.
You and your parents

Explain all your answers.

MEXICO

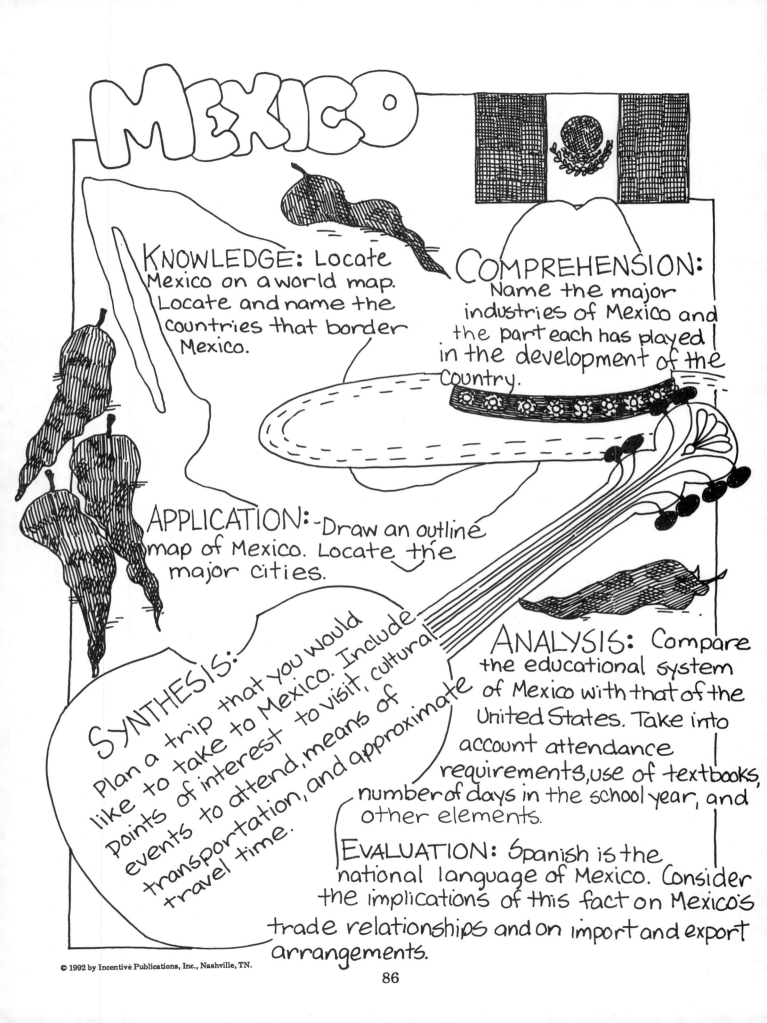

KNOWLEDGE: Locate Mexico on a world map. Locate and name the countries that border Mexico.

COMPREHENSION: Name the major industries of Mexico and the part each has played in the development of the country.

APPLICATION: -Draw an outline map of Mexico. Locate the major cities.

SYNTHESIS: Plan a trip that you would like to take to Mexico. Include points of interest to visit, cultural events to attend, means of transportation, and approximate travel time.

ANALYSIS: Compare the educational system of Mexico with that of the United States. Take into account attendance requirements, use of textbooks, number of days in the school year, and other elements.

EVALUATION: Spanish is the national language of Mexico. Consider the implications of this fact on Mexico's trade relationships and on import and export arrangements.

OLYMPIC GAMES

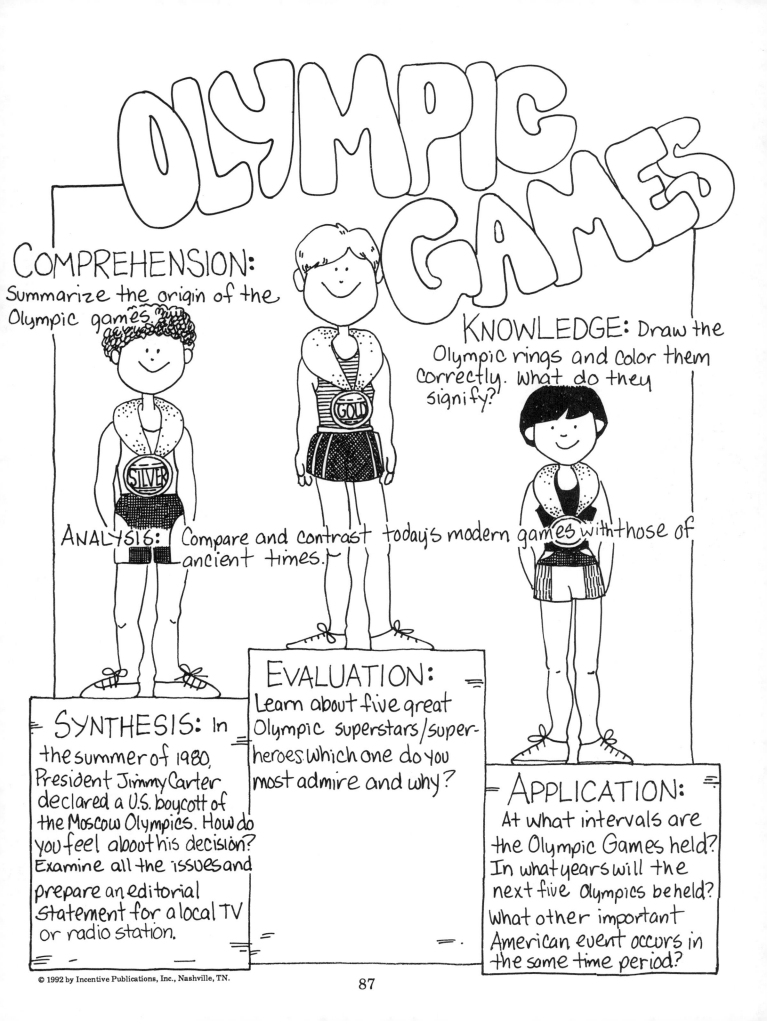

COMPREHENSION: Summarize the origin of the Olympic games.

KNOWLEDGE: Draw the Olympic rings and color them correctly. What do they signify?

ANALYSIS: Compare and contrast today's modern games with those of ancient times.

EVALUATION: Learn about five great Olympic superstars/super-heroes. Which one do you most admire and why?

SYNTHESIS: In the summer of 1980, President Jimmy Carter declared a U.S. boycott of the Moscow Olympics. How do you feel about his decision? Examine all the issues and prepare an editorial statement for a local TV or radio station.

APPLICATION: At what intervals are the Olympic Games held? In what years will the next five Olympics be held? What other important American event occurs in the same time period?

? QUESTIONING

KNOWLEDGE: Choose a scientific topic that is of interest to you. Write down five questions you would like to have answered about the topic.

COMPREHENSION: What are the best sources of information to use when looking for your answers? How will you begin your search?

APPLICATION: Perform an experiment related to your chosen topic. Use the scientific method.

SYNTHESIS: Design a poster for your science classroom. Include all the questioning words you can think of (who, how, etc.) and illustrate with a scientific motif.

ANALYSIS: Analyze your experiment to see if your hypothesis proved to be true. If it did not, what conclusions can you draw?

EVALUATION: Assess the importance of being a good questioner. Explain your answer.

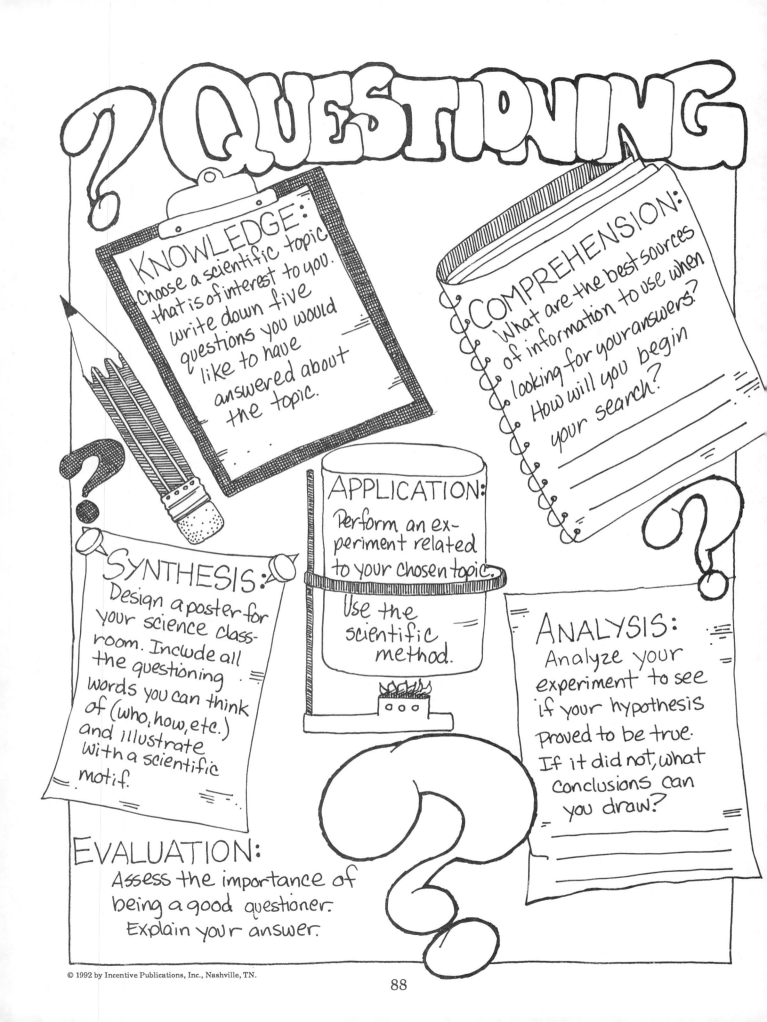

WEIGHT

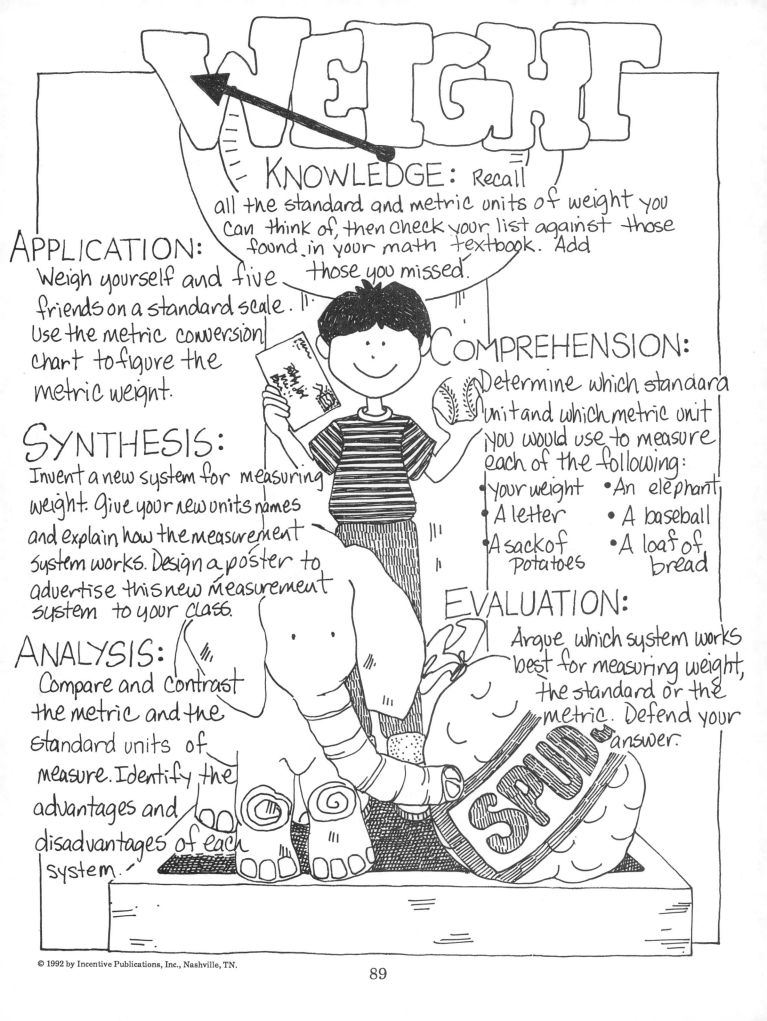

KNOWLEDGE: Recall all the standard and metric units of weight you can think of, then check your list against those found in your math textbook. Add those you missed.

APPLICATION: Weigh yourself and five friends on a standard scale. Use the metric conversion chart to figure the metric weight.

COMPREHENSION: Determine which standard unit and which metric unit you would use to measure each of the following:
- your weight
- A letter
- A sack of potatoes
- An elephant
- A baseball
- A loaf of bread

SYNTHESIS: Invent a new system for measuring weight. Give your new units names and explain how the measurement system works. Design a poster to advertise this new measurement system to your class.

ANALYSIS: Compare and contrast the metric and the standard units of measure. Identify the advantages and disadvantages of each system.

EVALUATION: Argue which system works best for measuring weight, the standard or the metric. Defend your answer.

SPUD

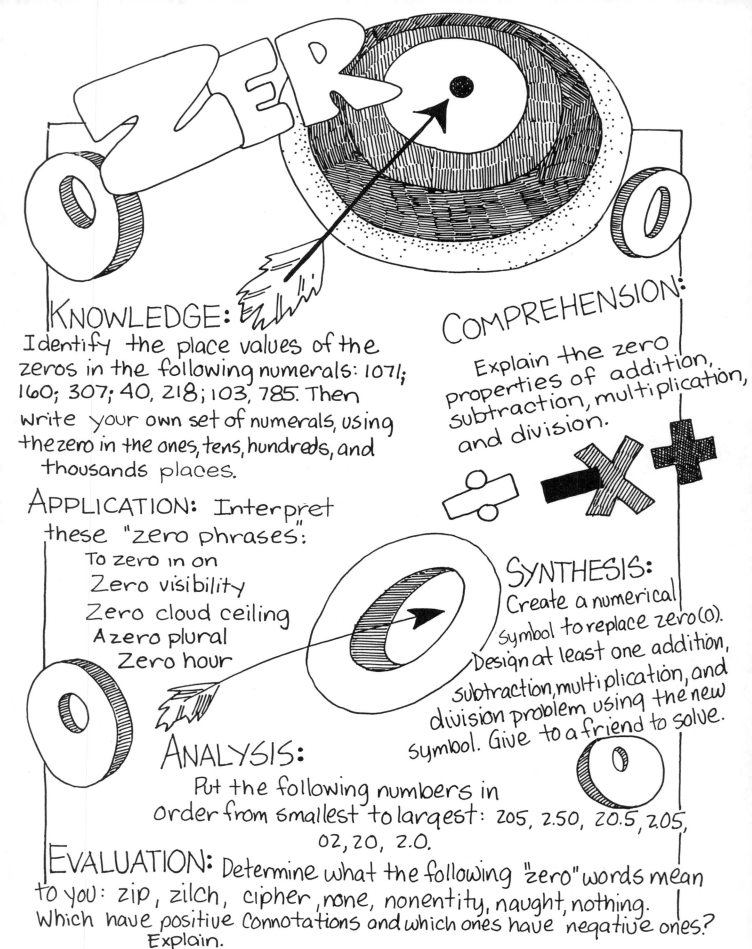

ZERO

KNOWLEDGE:
Identify the place values of the zeros in the following numerals: 1071; 160; 307; 40, 218; 103, 785. Then write your own set of numerals, using the zero in the ones, tens, hundreds, and thousands places.

APPLICATION:
Interpret these "zero phrases":
- To zero in on
- Zero visibility
- Zero cloud ceiling
- A zero plural
- Zero hour

COMPREHENSION:
Explain the zero properties of addition, subtraction, multiplication, and division.

SYNTHESIS:
Create a numerical symbol to replace zero (0). Design at least one addition, subtraction, multiplication, and division problem using the new symbol. Give to a friend to solve.

ANALYSIS:
Put the following numbers in order from smallest to largest: 205, 2.50, 20.5, 2.05, 02, 20, 2.0.

EVALUATION:
Determine what the following "zero" words mean to you: zip, zilch, cipher, none, nonentity, naught, nothing. Which have positive connotations and which ones have negative ones? Explain.

THEMATIC POSTER PROJECTS

PROJECT POSTER: EQUATIONS

PROJECT PLAN:

- Divide students into groups of four.
- Reproduce and distribute copies of student directions sheet and all four sections of the poster to each group.
- Provide pencils, markers or crayons, and paste, tape, or glue.
- Instruct groups to work together to complete the posters according to directions.
- Display completed poster on a bulletin board for the total group to critique and enjoy.

Project Poster: Equations

DIRECTIONS:

1. Select a Coordinator, Reader, Recorder, and Go-for.

2. Assemble your materials. You will need: four poster section pages, paste or glue, crayons or markers, and pencils. You may want to use scratch paper before putting individual work on the poster pages.

3. Work together to complete the poster.

4. Use markers to add interest to the poster.

5. Paste or tape the sections together to assemble the poster.

6. Display the poster for the total group to evaluate.

GROUP CHALLENGE:

Working as a group, come up with a list of examples of occupations that require frequent use of equations.

Name things which are equal.
For example: 36 inches = 1 yard
1 head + 1 body + 2 arms + 2 legs = 1 person

Label these statements T (true) or F (false).

_____ 0−7 = 7−0

_____ (12+6)+10=12+(6+10)

_____ (11−5)−4=11−(5−4)

_____ (7×6)×5=7×(6×5)

_____ (8−9)÷3=81÷(9÷3)

_____ 6−0=6

_____ 5÷1=5

_____ 8−0=0−8

_____ 3×6=6×3

_____ 1÷4=4÷1

Write an equation for doing well in school.

6+[6×6]×10=

A certain number plus 15 equals 63. What is the number?

Equation-

Solution-

The difference between a number and 25 is 48. What is the number?

Equation-

Solution-

Set up an equation for each problem and solve.

EQUATIONS

MC | M+ | M- | X | +
-

Determine all the reasons why you think someone invented equations. Rank them in order from most to least important. Explain.

Write an equation for good health.

If a certain number is divided by 4, the quotient is 17. What is the number?

equation –

Solution –

Mrs. Lewis is twice as old as her daughter, Mrs. Miller. Mrs. Miller is 23 years older than her daughter, Tricia. If Mrs. Lewis is 81, how old is Mrs. Miller? Tricia?

equation –

Solution –

START

$8 \times 3 + 3 \div 10 + 25$

PROJECT POSTER:
JUPITER

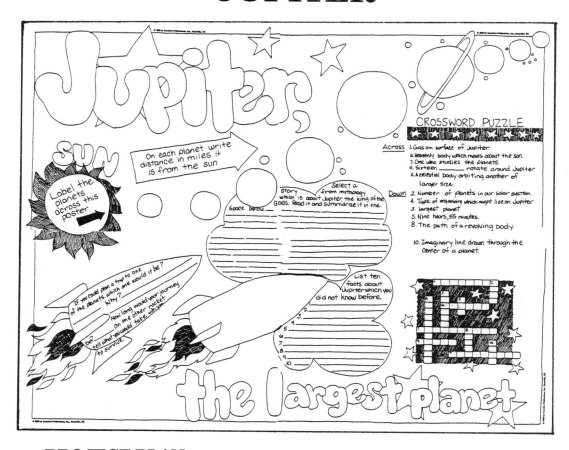

PROJECT PLAN:

- Divide students into groups of four.
- Reproduce and distribute copies of student directions sheet and all four sections of the poster to each group.
- Provide pencils, markers and crayons, and paste or glue.
- Instruct groups to work together to complete the posters according to directions.
- Display completed poster on a bulletin board for the total group to critique and enjoy.

Project Poster: Jupiter

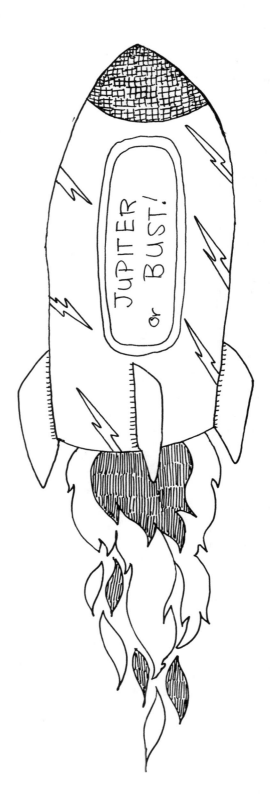

DIRECTIONS:

1. Select a Coordinator, Reader, Recorder, Researcher, and Go-for.

2. Assemble your materials. You will need: four poster section pages, paste or glue, crayons or markers, and pencils. You may want to use scratch paper before putting individual work on the poster pages.

3. Work together to complete the poster.

4. Use markers to add interest to the poster.

5. Paste or tape the sections together to assemble the poster.

6. Display the poster for the total group to evaluate.

GROUP CHALLENGE:

On a separate sheet of paper, draw the Roman god Jupiter's family tree.

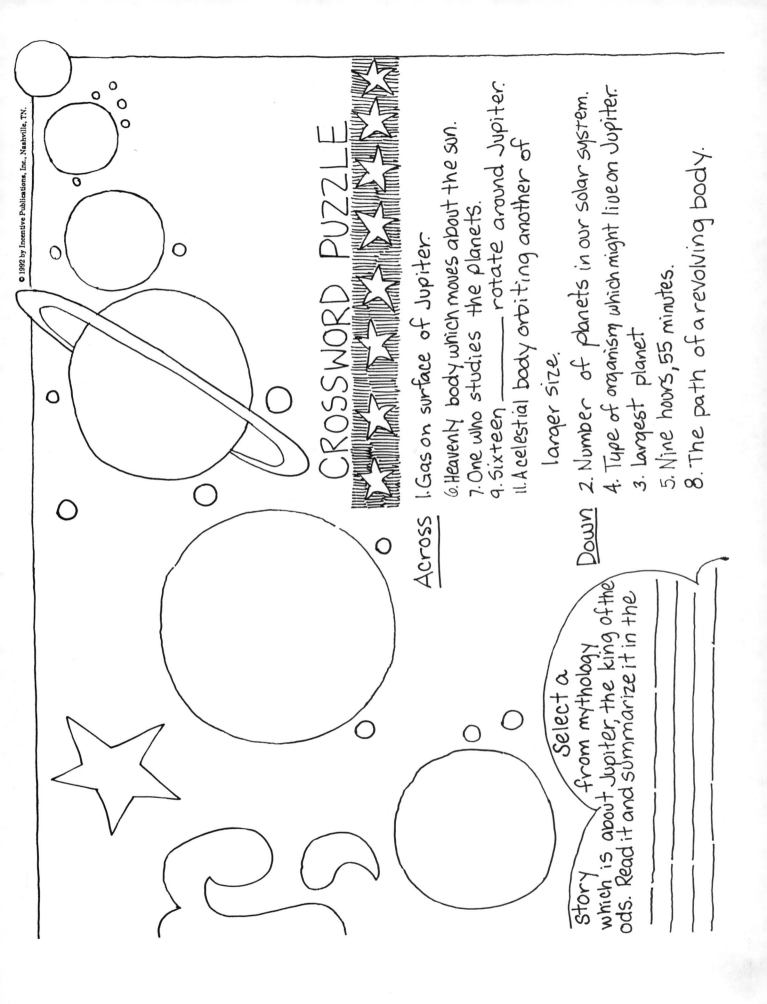

CROSSWORD PUZZLE

Across 1. Gas on surface of Jupiter.

6. Heavenly body which moves about the sun.
7. One who studies the planets.
9. Sixteen _____ rotate around Jupiter.
11. A celestial body orbiting another of larger size.

Down 2. Number of planets in our solar system.

4. Type of organism which might live on Jupiter.
3. Largest planet
5. Nine hours, 55 minutes.
8. The path of a revolving body.

Select a story from mythology which is about Jupiter, the king of the gods. Read it and summarize it in the

stars

On each planet write
distance in miles it
is from the sun

Space below. ____ G

SUN

Label the
planets this
across poster

the

If you could plan a trip to one of the planets, which one would it be? Why?

On the other rocket journey, tell what you would take with you to survive.

How long would your journey be?

10. Imaginary line drawn through the center of a planet.

List ten facts about Jupiter which you did not know before.

1.
2.
3.
4.
5.
6.
7.
8.
9.
10.

largest planet

PROJECT POSTER: NATIONAL PARKS

PROJECT PLAN:

- Divide students into groups of four.
- Reproduce and distribute copies of student directions sheet and all four sections of the poster to each group.
- Provide pencils, markers or crayons, and paste or tape.
- Instruct groups to work together to complete the posters according to directions.
- Display completed poster on a bulletin board for the total group to critique and enjoy.

Project Poster: National Parks

U.S. NATIONAL PARKS:

Everglades

Glacier

Shenandoah

Mammoth Cave

Carlsbad Caverns

Badlands

Yellowstone

Hot Springs

Wind Cave

Teddy Roosevelt

Grand Teton

North Cascades

Olympic

Mount Rainier

Crater Lake

Redwood

Lassen Volcanic

Yosemite

Rocky Mountain

Kings Canyon

Sequoia

Zion

Bryce Canyon

Capitol Reef

Canyonlands

Arches

Mesa Verde

Petrified Forest

Guadalupe Mountains

Big Bend

Biscayne

Great Smoky Mountain

DIRECTIONS:

1. Select a Coordinator, Reader, Recorder, Researcher, and Go-for.

2. Assemble your materials. You will need: four poster section pages, paste or glue, crayons or markers, and pencils. You may want to use scratch paper before putting individual work on the poster pages.

3. Work together to complete the poster.

4. Use names from the National Parks list. Locate them on the map by number. Try to add more to the map.

5. Use markers to add interest to the poster.

6. Paste or tape the sections together to assemble the poster.

7. Display the poster for the total group to evaluate.

GROUP CHALLENGE:

Put your heads together and, on a separate sheet of paper, design a poster promoting conservation of our national parks.

What manmade problems threaten our national parks? What measures are being taken to preserve the Parks?

National Parks

Complete this travel folder about a national park you would like to visit. Include pictures.

Outstanding features:

Price of admission:

Area:

Park Name:

Location:

Size:

If you
could nominate
a new area of the
country   a national
park, where would it
be? What would you
call it? What would you see
there?

Argue continued
acquisition of land for expanding
the national park system.
Defend your thoughts.

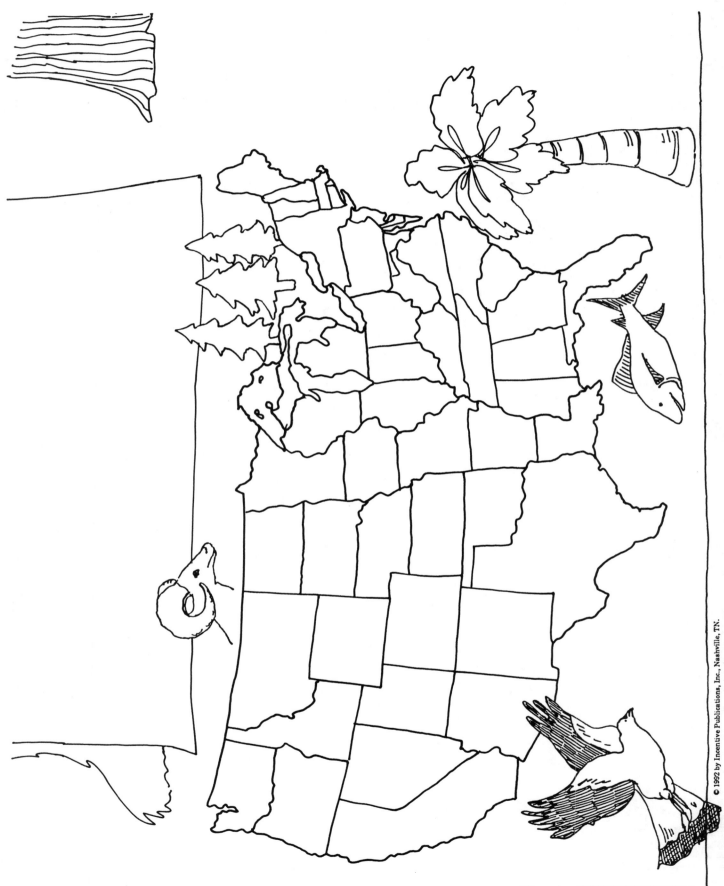

PROJECT POSTER: TEST-TAKING TIPS

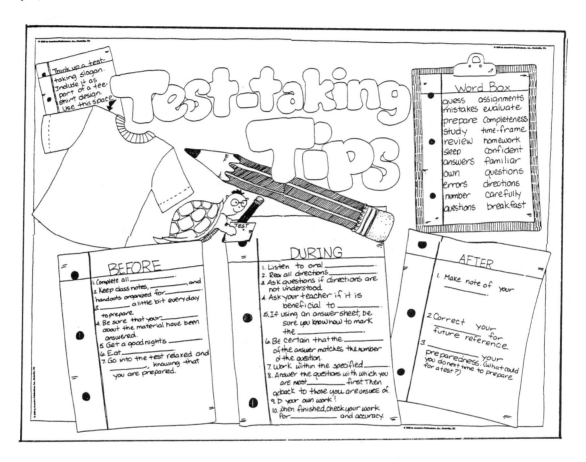

PROJECT PLAN:

- Divide students into groups of four.
- Reproduce and distribute copies of student directions sheet and all four sections of the poster to each group.
- Provide pencils, markers or crayons, and paste, tape, or glue.
- Instruct groups to work together to complete the posters according to directions.
- Display completed poster on a bulletin board for the total group to critique and enjoy.

Project Poster: Test-Taking Tips

guess	own	time-frame
mistakes	errors	homework
prepare	number	confident
study	questions	familiar
review	assignments	directions
sleep	completeness	carefully
answers	evaluate	breakfast

DIRECTIONS:

1. Select a Coordinator, Reader, Recorder, and Go-for.

2. Assemble your materials. You will need: four poster section pages, paste or glue, crayons or markers, and pencils. You may want to use scratch paper before putting individual work on the poster pages.

3. Work together to complete the poster.

4. Use words from the Word Box to fill in the blanks.

5. Add additional tips in spaces indicated.

6. Use markers to add interest to the poster.

7. Paste or tape the sections together to complete the poster.

8. Discuss the tips and their significance to your group.

9. Display the poster for the total group to evaluate.

GROUP CHALLENGE:

Brainstorm more interesting words with the same meaning to substitute for as many words as possible in the Word Box. A dictionary or thesaurus will help.

Taking Tests

Word Box

guess	assignments	
mistakes	evaluate	
prepare	Completeness	
Study	time-frame	
review	homework	
sleep	confident	
answers	familiar	
own	questions	
errors	directions	
number	carefully	
questions	breakfast	

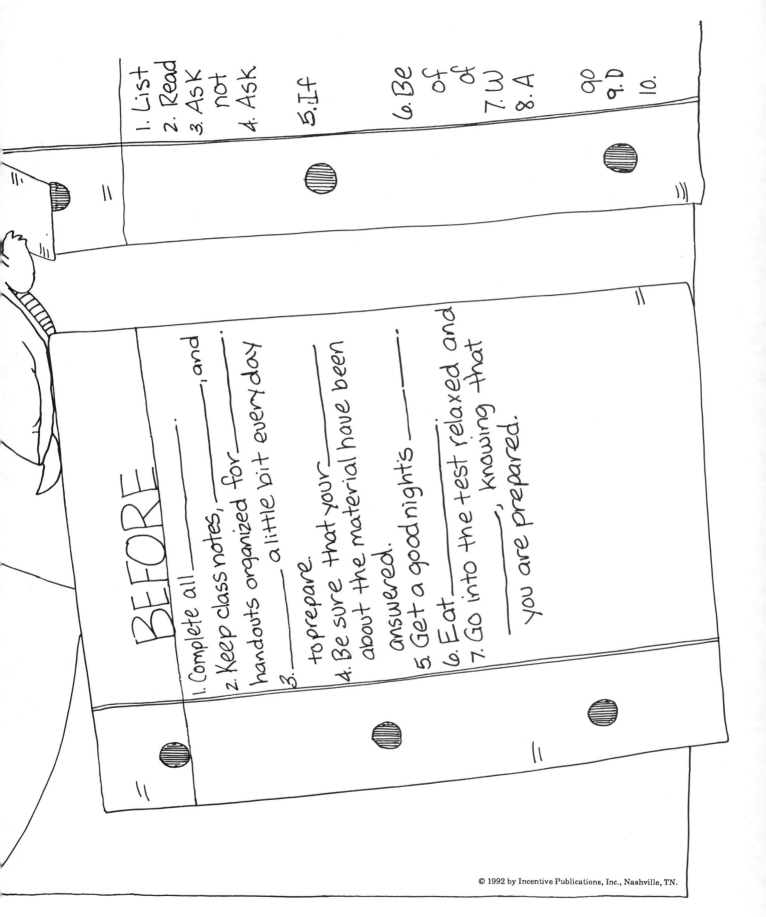

BEFORE

1. Complete all _____, and _____.
2. Keep class notes, _____, and handouts organized for _____.
   _____ a little bit every day _____
3. _____ to prepare.
4. Be sure that your _____ about the material have been _____ answered.
5. Get a good nights _____.
6. Eat _____.
7. Go into the test relaxed and _____, knowing that _____ you are prepared.

1. List
2. Read
3. Ask
   not
4. Ask

5. If

6. Be
   of
   of
7. W
8. A

9. O
9. D
10.

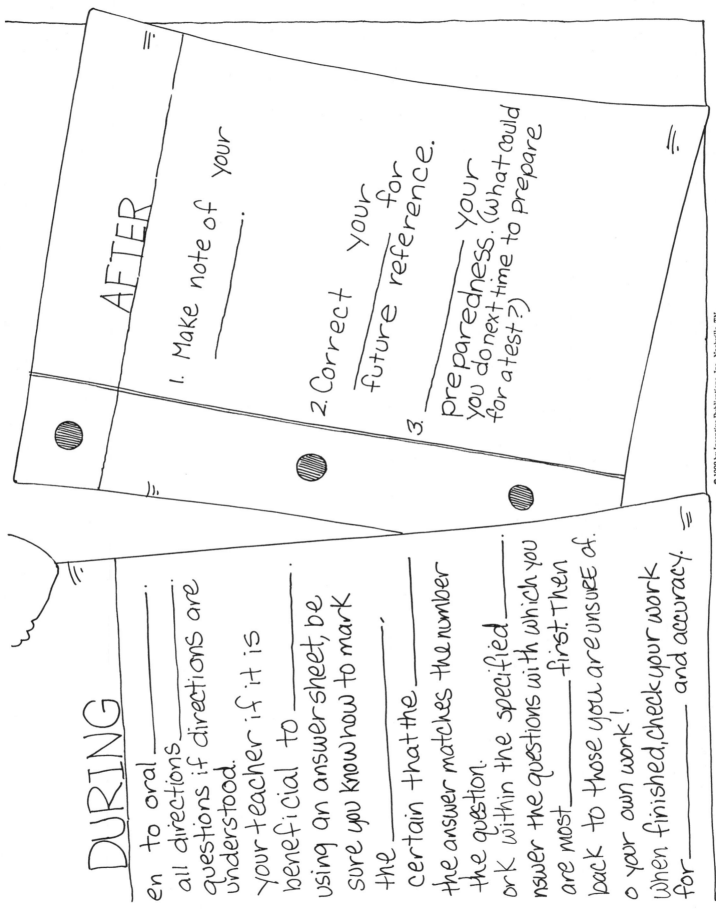

AFTER

1. Make note of your _____ .

2. Correct your _____ for future reference.

3. _____ preparedness. Your _____ (What could you do next time to prepare for a test?)

DURING

____en to oral _____ all directions
_____ questions if directions are understood.

_____ your teacher if it is beneficial to _____ .

using an answer sheet, be sure you know how to mark the _____ .

_____ certain that the _____ the answer matches the number the question.

____ork within the specified _____

____nswer the questions with which you _____ first. Then _____ are most _____ back to those you are unsure of.

___o your own work!

When finished, check your work for _____ and accuracy.

PROJECT POSTER: VOLCANOES

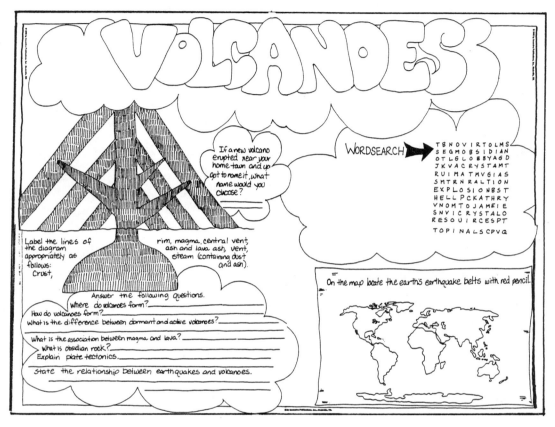

PROJECT PLAN:

- Divide students into groups of four.
- Reproduce and distribute copies of student directions sheet and all four sections of the poster to each group.
- Provide pencils, markers or crayons, and paste or tape.
- Instruct groups to work together to complete the posters according to directions.
- Display completed poster on a bulletin board for the total group to critique and enjoy.

Project Poster: Volcanoes

FAMOUS VOLCANOES OF THE WORLD:

Mount Vesuvius   Mount St. Helens
Mount Etna   Mauna Loa
Mount Fuji   Mount Hood
Kilimanjaro   Paracutín

DIRECTIONS:

1. Select a Coordinator, Reader, Recorder, Researcher, and Go-for.

2. Assemble your materials. You will need: four poster section pages, paste or glue, crayons or markers, and pencils. You may want to use scratch paper before putting individual work on the poster pages.

3. Work together to complete the poster.

4. Use names from the Famous Volcanoes of the World list. Locate them on the map by number. Try to add more to the map.

5. Use markers to add interest to the poster.

6. Paste or tape the sections together to complete the poster.

7. Display the poster for the total group to evaluate.

GROUP CHALLENGE:

Make a group visit to the site of a famous volcano. Working as a group, design a postcard with a message that has something to do with your visit. If you prefer, you may design individual postcards, then choose the best one to represent your group's work.

Label the lines of the diagram appropriately as follows:
Crust, rim, magma, central vent, ash and lava ash, vent, steam (containing dust and ash).

Answer the following questions.

Where do volcanoes form? _____

How do volcanoes form? _____

What is the difference between dormant and active volcanoes? _____

What is the association between magma and lava? _____

What is obsidian rock? _____

Explain plate tectonics. _____

State the relationship between earthquakes and volcanoes. _____

TOPINALSCPVQ

On the map locate the earth's earthquake belts with red pencil.

TEACHER'S TOOL KIT

Student Worksheets

Thematic Things To Do When There's Nothing To Do

THINKING GLOBALLY

With the total group, choose a day to celebrate as "Global Awareness Day." Brainstorm ways in which the group might become involved in activities that will increase global awareness. The following are suggestions to spark the brainstorming discussion:

- Arrange a classroom display of books on cultures of many countries. Students may bring books and magazines from home, and also scout the library for appropriate selections. Quality of illustrations and authenticity of information should be understood as helping to ensure a truly informative collection.
- In the same way, assemble an international artifact collection.
- Write to the United Nations Information Center for materials and information.
- Make a list of people in the school or community who have special expertise on certain countries and/or cultures.
- Make a list of "global awareness" movies or videos that the class could procure.
- Collect and learn songs and games from other countries.

After the brainstorming session, divide the group into small groups of not less than four and not more than six to plan an international festival. Each group will be responsible for researching one country and should plan to "present" the country at the festival. When doing research, each group should consider its country's history, industries, location and climate, clothing, food, and customs. The groups should then plan festival displays representative of their research. Each display could perhaps include the country's flag, map of the country, costumes and/or other artifacts, brochures, posters, and even food samples if possible. Spokespersons for each display should be appointed to serve on a rotating basis so that someone is always present to explain the contents of the display.

As a culminating activity, after students have had ample opportunity to visit all displays, each group may make an organized presentation to add to the festivities. Skits, creative dance, songs, games, puppet shows, and panels are some possibilities. Groups are sure to think of ideas of their own. A marvelous memory-making day will be the result of group interaction, planning, and follow-through.

2, 4, 6, 8, WHO DO WE APPRECIATE?

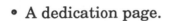

Have students work in groups of no more than four to select a special person in the school or community to honor. Students should then plan a special appreciation booklet to present to the chosen person. Provide paper for booklets, construction paper for covers, pens, pencils, and markers or crayons.

The booklet should include components such as the following:

- A dedication page.

- "The funniest thing we remember about _____ is ..."

- "If we could give _____ something special, it would be ..."

- "A favorite thing about _____ is . . ."

- "The thing we will always remember most about _____ is ..."

- Other pages about the person's unique history and qualities.

- A closing page.

The pages and cover should be creatively illustrated. After the booklets are completed and taken home, a class period should be designated for sharing the booklets before they are presented.

It might be fun, too, to set aside a brief amount of time to discuss reactions of the booklet recipients after they have been delivered.

PERSONALIZING MATH

To promote creative thinking and extend understanding of math concepts, divide students into small groups and have them discuss individual responses to one or more of these questions:

- Are you more like a square or a circle?
- Are you more like a compass or a protractor?
- Are you more like a decimal or a fraction?
- Are you more like a calculator or a computer?
- Are you more like addition or subtraction?
- Are you more like a gram or a pound?

Instruct students to give two good reasons for each response.

Ask each group to then develop a list of questions with a scientific focus. At another time, the groups may exchange lists.

A DIFFERENT DRUMMER

"IF A MAN DOES NOT KEEP PACE WITH HIS COMPANIONS, PERHAPS IT IS BECAUSE HE HEARS A DIFFERENT DRUMMER. LET HIM STEP TO THE MUSIC WHICH HE HEARS, HOWEVER MEASURED OR FAR AWAY."

—Henry David Thoreau

Divide students into groups of three or four to react to this statement by discussing the following questions:

- Do you agree or disagree with this statement? Why?
- Come up with the names of some people who have "stepped to the beat of a different drummer." What effects might this way of living have had on the world? On the individual?
- Is this idea something you would like your own children to believe?

At the conclusion of the small group sessions, one member of each group should be elected (by group vote) to act as spokesperson for the group. The elected spokespersons should then serve as panel members to summarize and present the small group conclusions to the total group.

CONFLICT CONSIDERATION

Have students work in teams of three to discuss conflicts in their lives. Ask each student to present for discussion one particular conflict that is especially troubling at the present time. The other two students are to listen attentively and objectively. They then should act as "conflict clarifiers," giving insights to the problems as they see them and making suggestions for resolution of the conflict.

After each of the three conflicts has been fully discussed, each student is to write a letter to the person with whom the conflict is occurring. Supply the following guidelines for letter-writing:

- Address the person courteously.

- State the problem as you see it.

- State how this conflict affects you personally.

- State how you would like the situation to be resolved.

- State what you are willing to do to help resolve the conflict, when you will do it, and how you will do it.

- Ask the person for cooperation and/or for other suggestions for resolving the conflict and for a reply to your letter.

Ask students to criticize one another's letters to determine if the conflict has been stated objectively and the suggestions for resolution appear to be advantageous to both parties. After the critique, leave the decision to deliver the letters or not up to each individual.

MATH FAIR

Engage the total group in planning a Math Fair. Have a brainstorming session to determine the concept and purpose of a Math Fair; list the major objectives on the blackboard. Discuss the time and space requirements for preparation and presentation, and determine the date, time, and place for the fair. Continue the discussion to establish the overall theme that will be in keeping with the group's interest and will also lend itself to the time and space restrictions. Decide if parents and/or other classes or groups will be invited to the fair, and, if so, make plans for issuing the invitations and extending hospitality. Continue the total group discussion to determine the award levels to be presented (1st, 2nd, 3rd place or Most Outstanding, Most Comprehensive, Most Original, etc.).

After the overall guidelines have been set, divide the students into small groups to assume responsibility for planning and carrying out the following tasks:

- Determining guidelines for setting up a booth or display.
- Determining topics, demonstrations, projects that could be presented, and establishing criteria for presentation.
- Developing a marketing plan to get students involved.
- Developing types of awards or contests to be included.
- Evaluating its success or lack of success.
- Establishing a public relations plan for gaining community support for the fair.

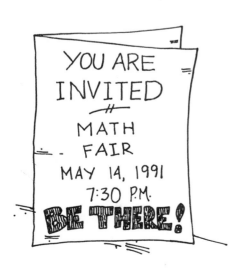

Small-group responsibility should include the preparation of written guides, awards, press notices, posters, and other materials necessary for carrying out the function of the group. Two or three total group discussions with supporting small group work sessions will be required as plans develop. Both small and total group post-fair sessions should be planned for evaluation of overall effectiveness, group interaction, and support.

"BEE" SHARP!

Divide the class into small groups. Ask each group to select a topic (math, science, current events, history, geography, sports, spelling) for its "bee." Each group should generate a list of questions that go with its chosen topic. The lists can then be put into a hat, to be drawn at random as time permits.

When a list is drawn, the originating group will be responsible for conducting a "bee" in which the entire class will participate. If desired, elements other than questions may be included on the lists: terms to define, concepts to explain, tasks to perform, etc.

THE PERFECT FIELD TRIP

Have students work in small groups to decide on "the perfect field trip" for the class. Ask students to determine:

- Objectives for the trip.
- Destination.
- Necessary preparations.
- Budgetary requirements.
- Date, time, and method of transportation.
- Plan for action on site.
- Possible problems that could be encountered, and ways to overcome the problems.
- Method of evaluation in terms of established objectives.

Direct each small group to conclude the discussion by preparing a written overview of the trip. The overview should take into account the guidelines listed above, and should be presented to the entire group. Allow the total group to vote on "the perfect field trip" and, if at all possible, to carry it out.

HAVE YOU HEARD?

Divide the students into groups of four or five. Seat students in a circle. Ask one student to start the "Have You Heard?" game by whispering in the ear of the student to the right one or two facts about the student to the left. Example: "Julie has red hair and beautiful green eyes." The game continues with each student repeating the whispered information aloud and then whispering a new fact about the student to the left which is then added to the database being passed along. Example: "Julie has red hair and beautiful green eyes. Sam has big feet and likes to wear boots and a cowboy hat. Jerry wants to be an airline pilot and fly to every country in the world," etc. The last person in the group will repeat all the information aloud and add, "and I ...., " adding one fact about himself or herself.

The game may then begin again after all players have changed places in the circle so that new facts about each person are supplied by a different person. Groups may also be combined after the second round to allow for larger group interaction.

This is a great "get-acquainted" game for the first week of school.

GO THAT EXTRA CENTIMETER!

Ask the students to assume that the President of the United States has just issued a proclamation that makes the metric system the official standard of measure to be used throughout the nation. Divide the class into small groups, and ask each to create a billboard design announcing this change to the citizens.

Charge each group with discussing the consequences of such a proclamation and the influence it would have on daily life in their own community as well as nationally. Display the completed billboard designs on a bulletin board to spark further discussion.

CHANGING TIME!

Have students re-create the calendar.

This is a good "imagination stretcher," and also promotes original thinking. Divide the class into small groups, and assign each group a different month. Instruct them to put their "thinking caps" on and to "invent" new holidays to replace the ones that already exist in their month. Have each group decide on a date for each holiday, what traditions they will observe, what type of greeting cards and messages they will compose to observe the holiday, as well as what type of refreshments would be appropriate.

An added treat would be to have the total group vote on their favorite "imaginary" holiday, and observe it as drawn up by the originating group. This could result in a classroom celebration with extraordinary flair.

COLORAMA

Divide students into small groups and give each group a different color. Have them collectively create a series of color poems using any of these formats: haiku, diamante, free verse, tanka, limerick, rhyming couplets.

Provide paper and art supplies so that the completed "coloramas" can be illustrated.

NATIONAL PET PEEVE DAY

Ask students to pretend that it is National Pet Peeve Day.

Divide the class into small groups. Ask each group to brainstorm a list of their collective pet peeves. Each group should then determine their "greatest peeve of all," and design a banner to display this "pet peeve" in a creative manner.

After the banners have been completed and displayed, set aside time for each group to read their entire list of "pet peeves" to the total group. From the lists presented, through discussion or democratic vote select the "greatest peeve of all."

This activity could be narrowed to a more specific focus by limiting the "pet peeves" to one particular subject such as pet peeves about school rules, pet peeves about TV programs, the class newspaper, homework assignments, etc.

UP WITH MATH

Involve the total group in developing a proclamation to establish a date for MATH LITERACY DAY to promote math awareness to the entire school population. Ask students to work in groups of two to develop posters for school-wide display to draw attention to the campaign, and to encourage awareness of the need for improved math skills and concepts in everyday life.

Guide For Studying The Life Of A Person

Full Name of Person: _____

Date and Place of Birth: _____

Date and Place of Death (if deceased): _____

Reasons for Studying Person's Life (major achievements or contributions): _____

_____

_____

Facts about early life, education, hobbies, occupations: _____

_____

_____

_____

_____

_____

_____

_____

Brief biographical sketch: _____

_____

_____

_____

_____

_____

WORLD MAP

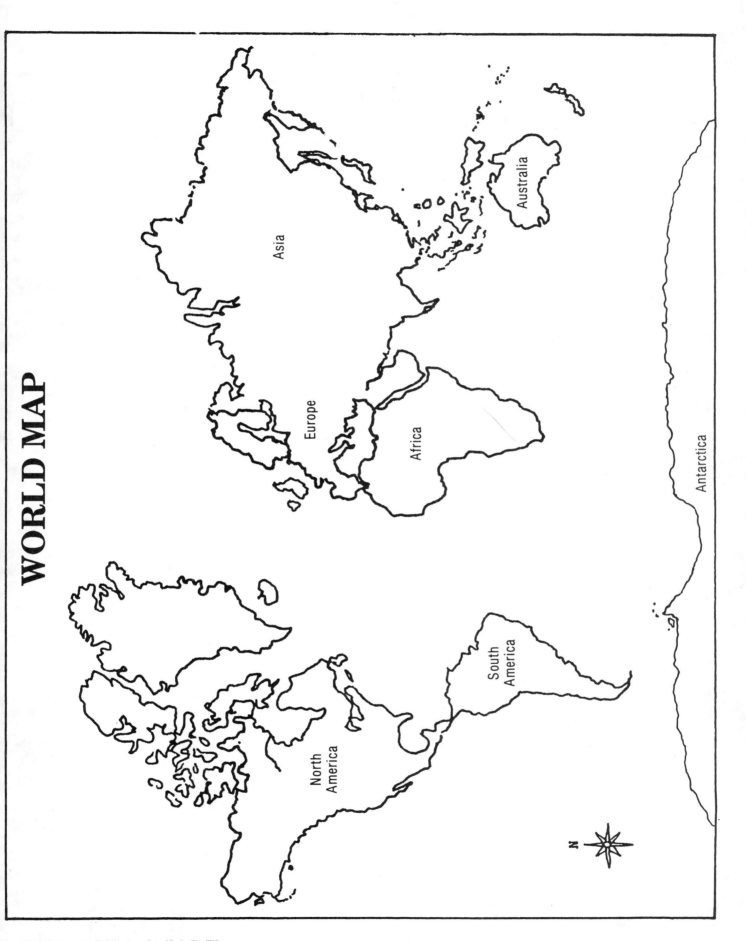

Asia

Australia

Europe

Africa

Antarctica

North America

South America

N

Name _____   Date _____

Guide For Studying A Country

Name of Country: _____

Three Distinctive Features of the Country (size, shape, location, etc.): _____
_____
_____
_____

Brief Statement of Early History (when, where, how, and by whom it was settled): _____
_____
_____
_____

Was the country governed by another country at one time? _____

If so, name the mother country. _____

Is the country now independent? _____

If so, in what year did it gain independence? _____

Name a well-known person from the country and tell what the person is known for.

_____
_____

Sketch of Outline Map of Country: Sketch of Country's Flag:

THOUGHT-A-DAY CALENDAR

SUNDAY	MONDAY	TUESDAY	WEDNESDAY	THURSDAY	FRIDAY	SATURDAY

Group Project Plan

Activity: _____

Group Members: Role Assignments:

_____   _____

_____   _____

_____   _____

_____   _____

_____   _____

Beginning Date:_____   Completion Date: _____

Materials Needed: _____

_____

_____

_____

Major Objective: _____

_____

_____

Specific Learning Goals: _____

_____

_____

_____

Plan Of Action: _____

_____

_____

_____

Group Rating Scale

Activity _____

	Excellent	Good	Fair	Poor
Group Interaction				
Individual Contributions				
Role Assignments				
Objectives				
Plan Of Action				
Materials				
Use Of Time				
Overall Rating				

Signatures:

_____   _____

_____   _____

_____   _____

_____   Date: _____

Group Evaluation

Activity: _____

Group Interaction: _____
_____

Individual Contributions: _____
_____

Effectiveness Of Objectives: _____
_____

Effectiveness Of Action Plan: _____
_____

Applicability Of Materials Selected: _____
_____

Use Of Time: _____
_____

Major Problems: _____
_____
_____

Major Strengths: _____
_____
_____

Summary: _____
_____
_____

Next Time We Would: _____
_____

Signatures: _____ _____
_____ _____
_____ _____

Date: _____

BIBLIOGRAPHY

Breeden, T. and Mosley, J. *The Middle Grades Teacher's Handbook for Cooperative Learning*. Nashville, TN: Incentive Publications, 1991.

Cohen, E.G. *Designing Groupwork: Strategies for the Heterogeneous Classroom*. New York: Teachers College Press, 1986.

Ellis, S.S. and Whalen, S.F. *Cooperative Learning Getting Started*. Jefferson City, MO: Scholastic Professional Books, 1990.

Farnette, C., Forte, I., and Loss, B. *People Need Each Other (Revised)*. Nashville: Incentive Publications, 1989.

Forte, I. and MacKenzie, J. *Pulling Together For Cooperative Learning*. Nashville: Incentive Publications, 1991.

Forte, I. and Schurr, S. *Science Mind Stretchers*. Nashville: Incentive Publications, 1987.

Jacobs, H.H. *How To Integrate the Curriculum*. Palatine, IL: Skylight Publishing, 1991.

Jacobs, H.H., Ed. *Interdisciplinary Curriculum: Design and Implementation*. Alexandria, VA: Association for Supervision and Curriculum Development, 1989.

Johnson, D.W., and Johnson, R. *Circles of Learning (2nd edition)*. Edina, MN: Interaction Book Company, 1986.

Johnson, D.W., and Johnson, R. *Learning Together and Alone: Cooperation, Competition, and Individualization (2nd edition)*. Englewood Cliffs, NJ: Prentice-Hall, 1987.

Johnson, D.W., Johnson, R.T., and Holubec, E.J. *Circles of Learning: Cooperation in the Classroom (Revised)*. Edina: Interaction Book Company, 1986.

Vars, Gordon F. *Interdisciplinary Teaching in the Middle Grades: Why and How*. Columbus, OH: National Middle School Association, 1987.

INDEX